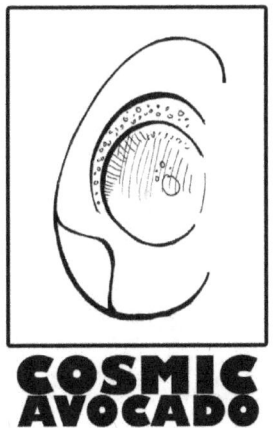

COSMIC
AVOCADO

# ANIMALS

## COLORING WITH FRANK : VOLUME II

## ART BY FRANK LOUIS ALLEN

### DESIGN BY COSMIC AVOCADO
### @ FRANKDRAWS.COM

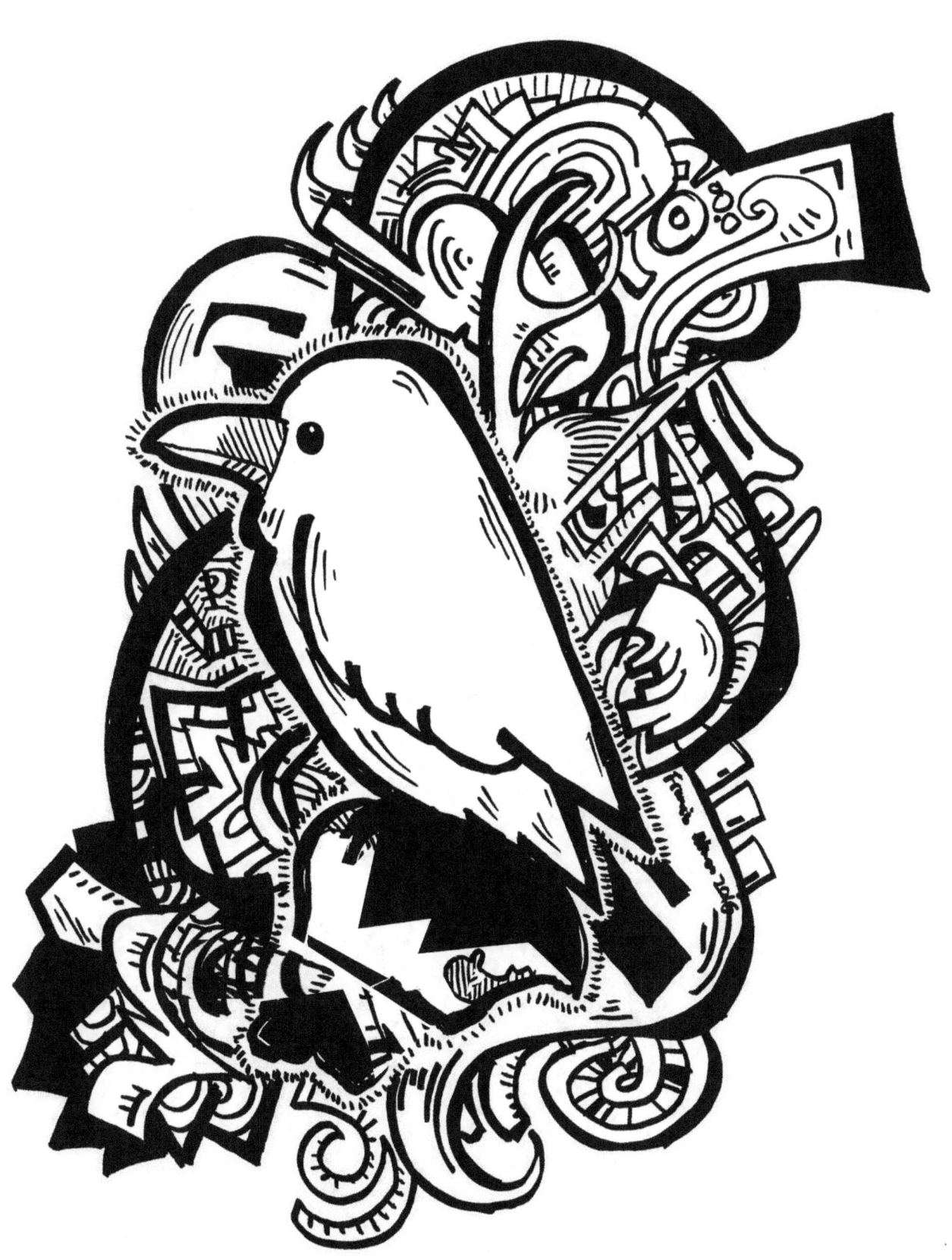

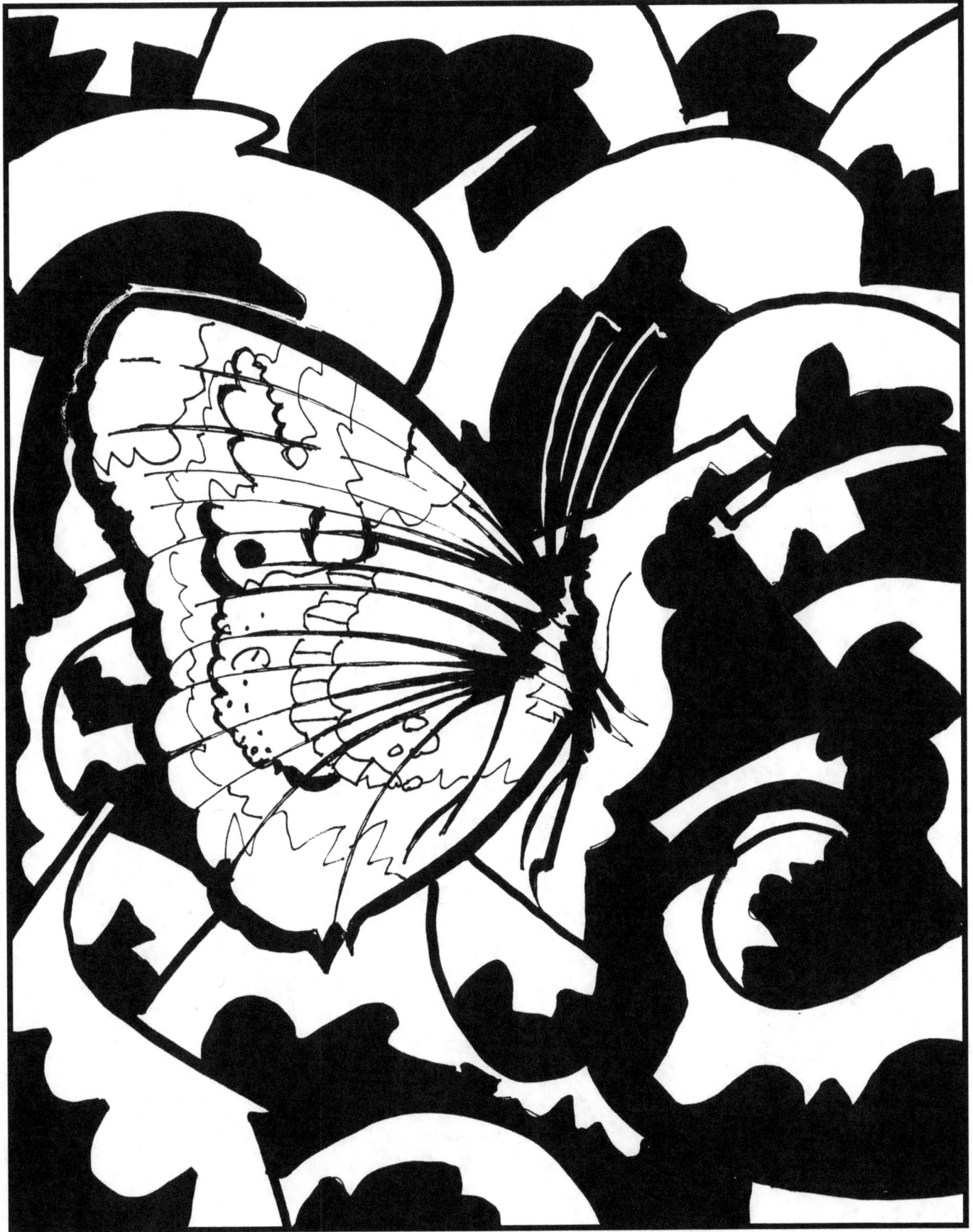

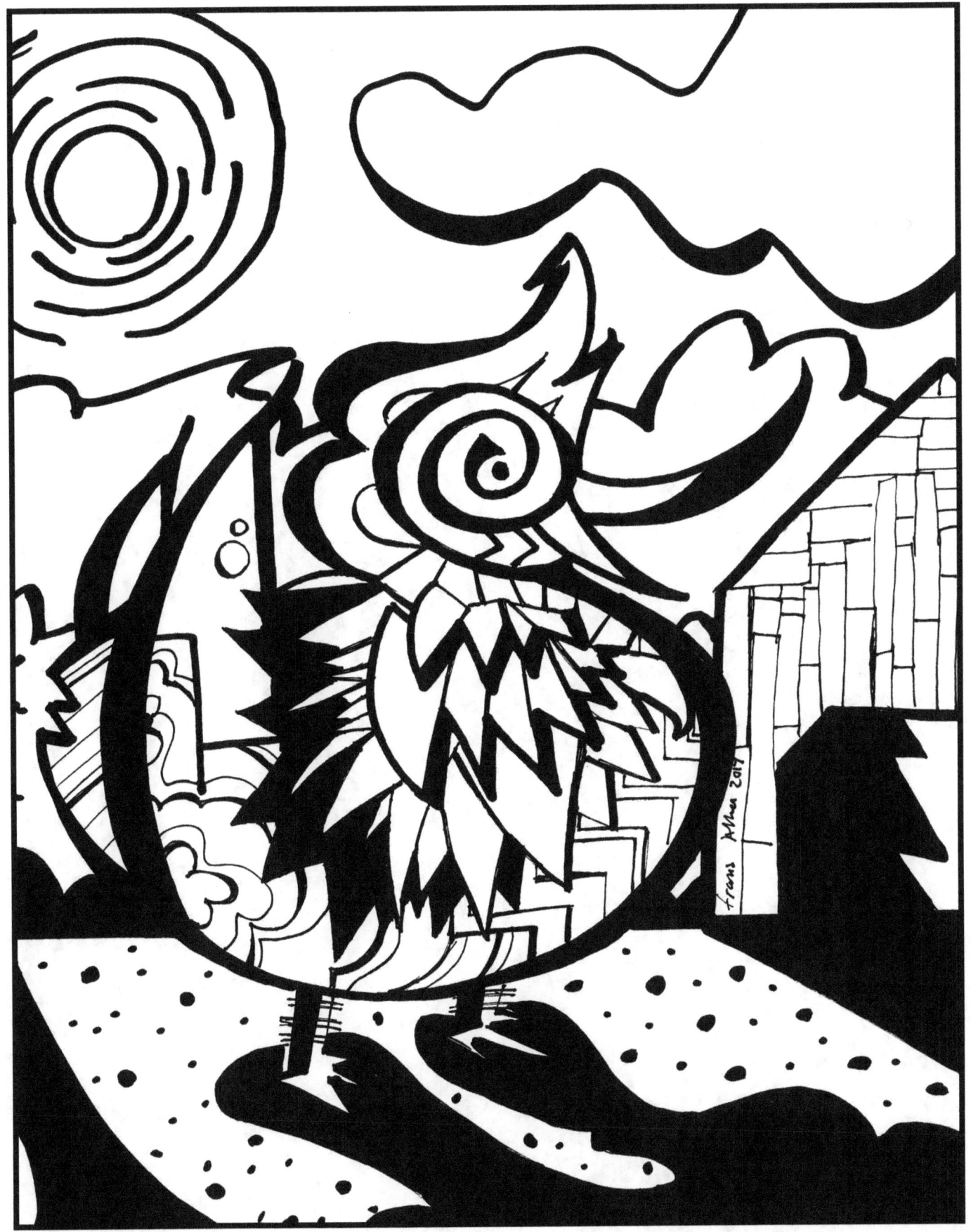

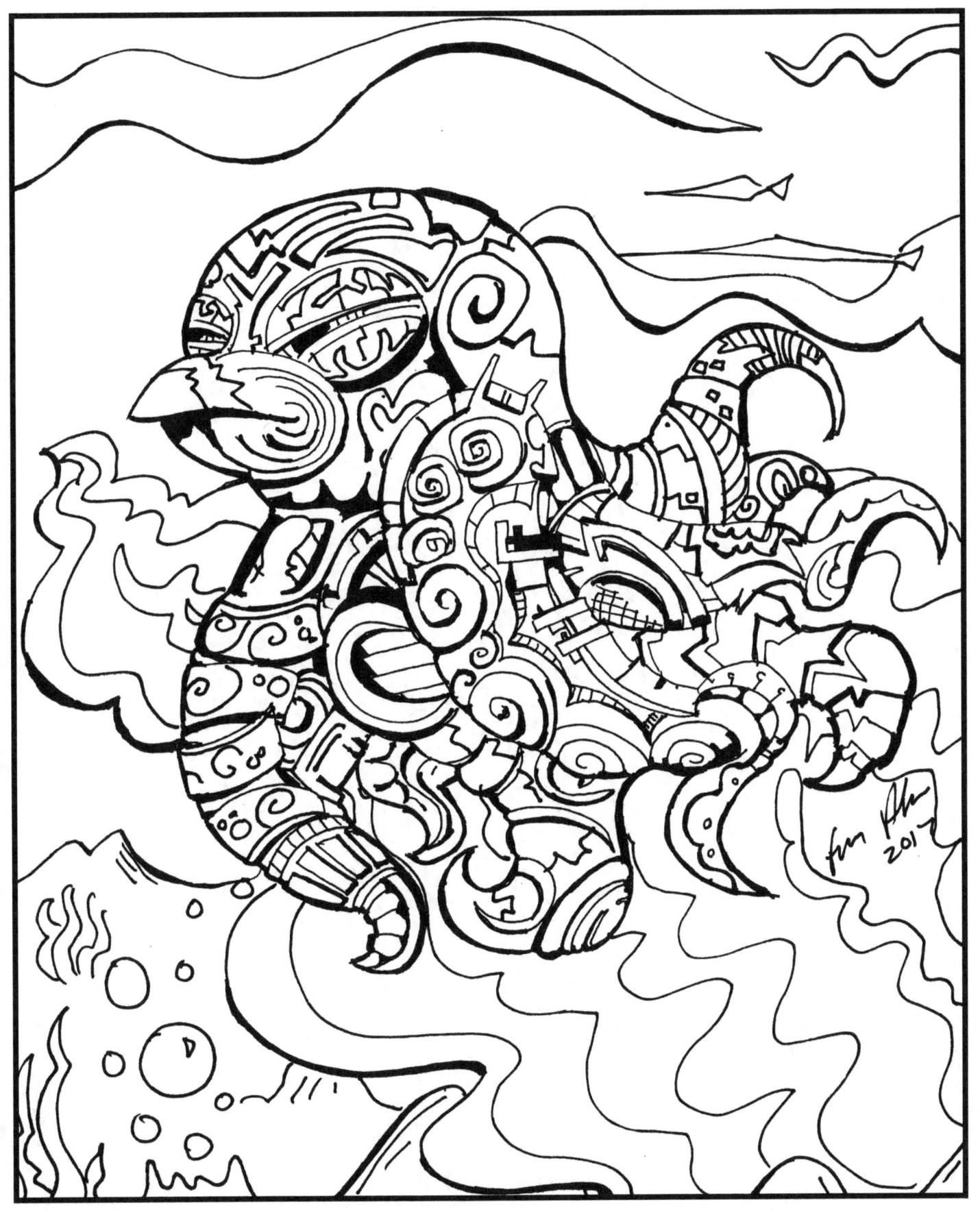

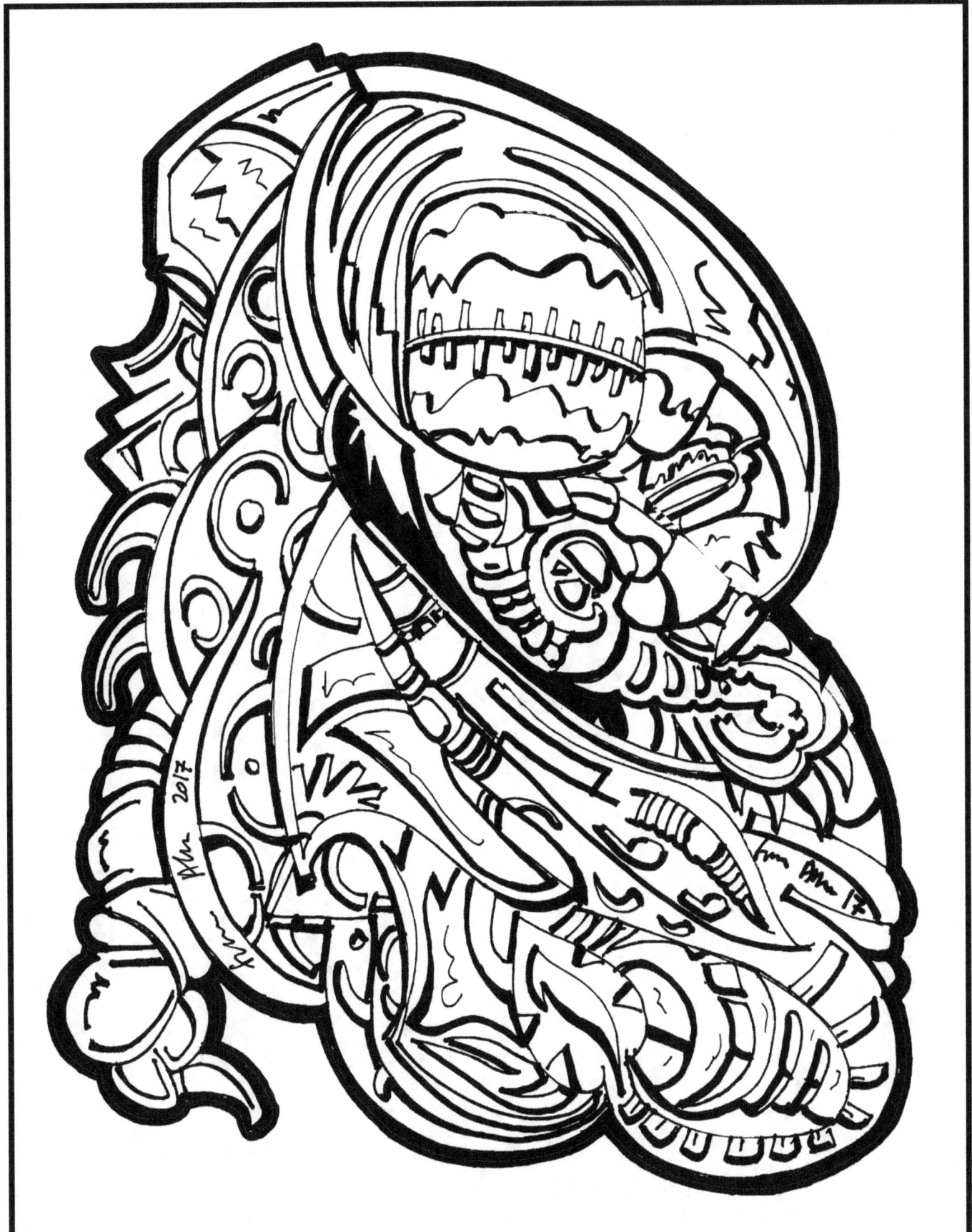

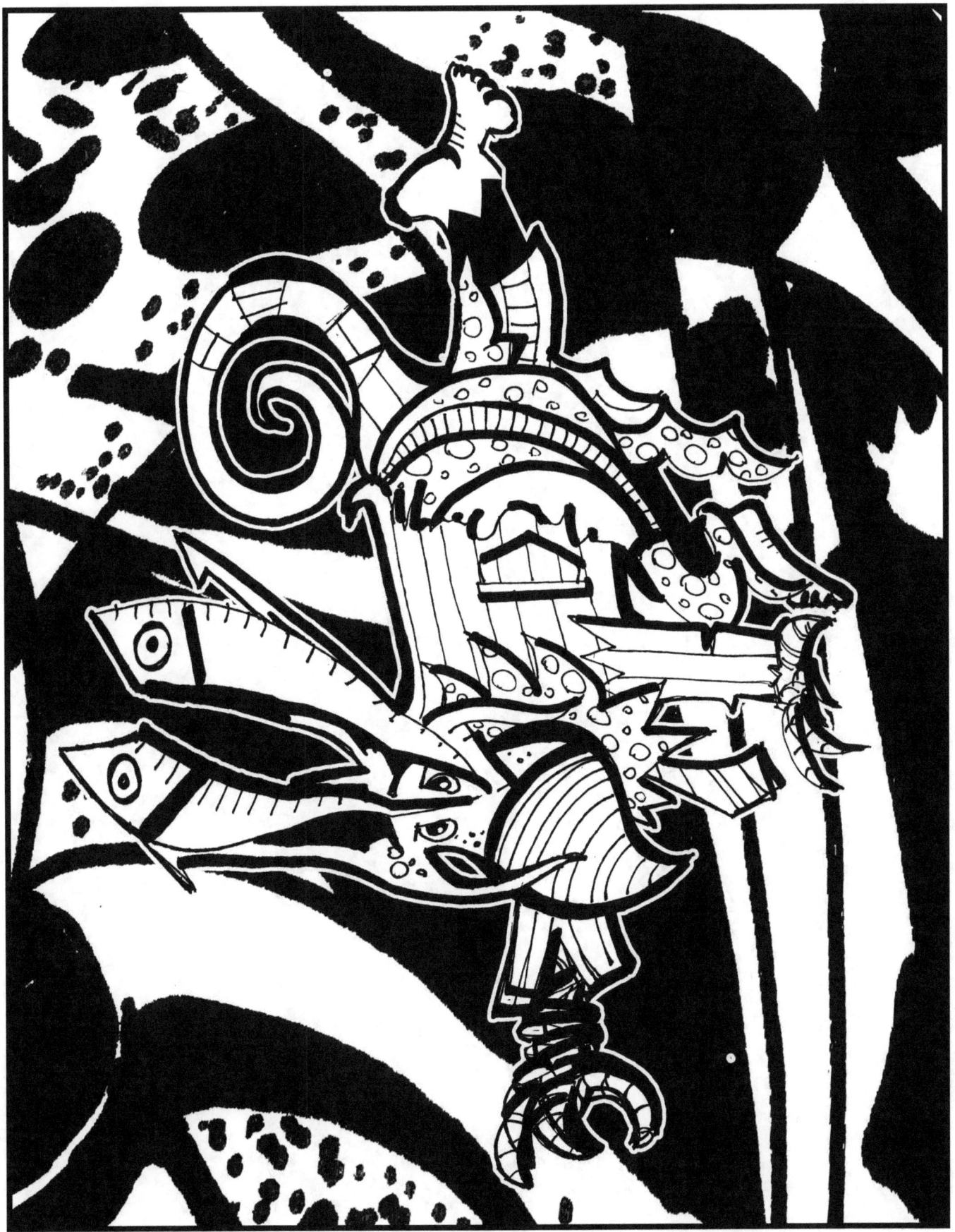

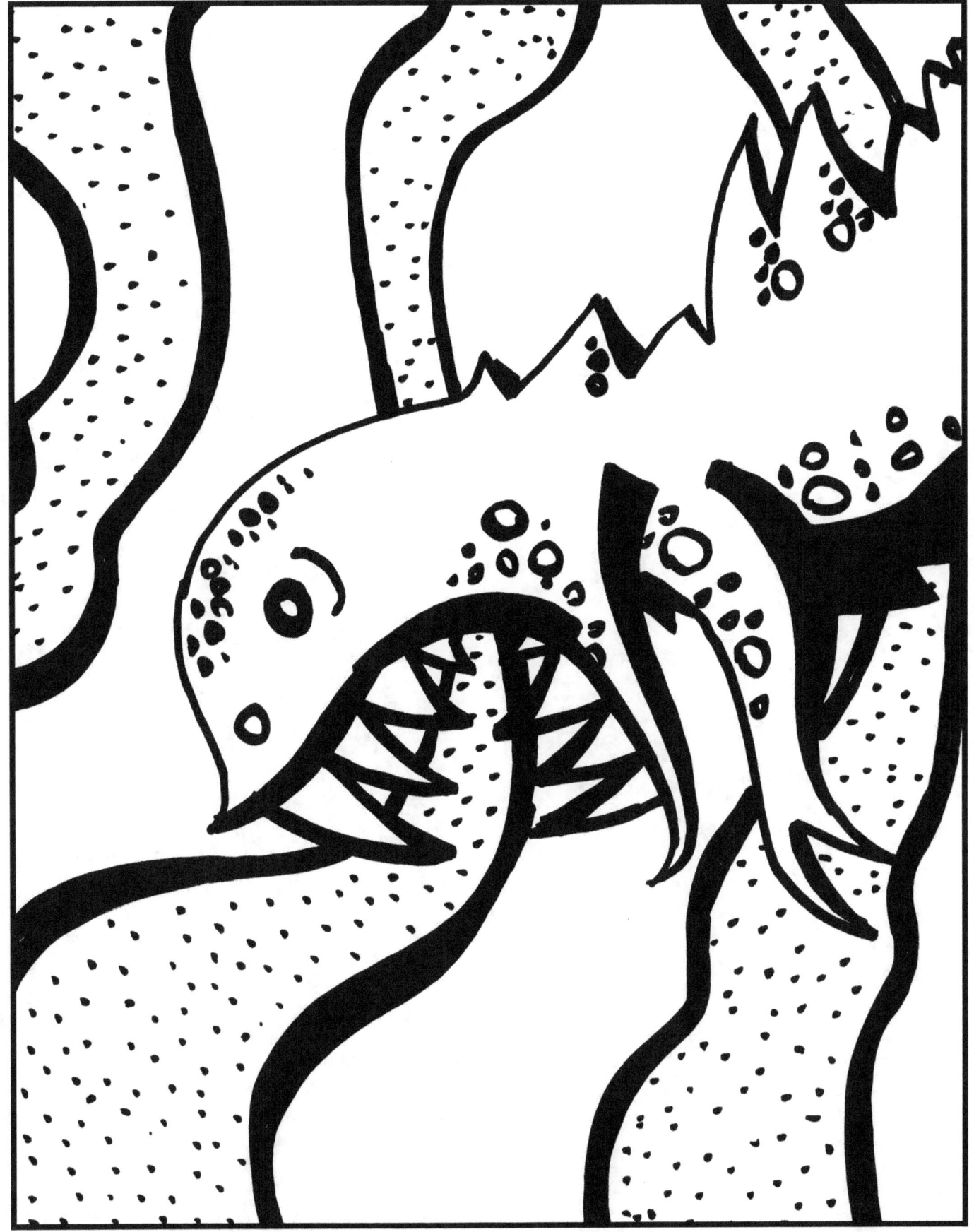

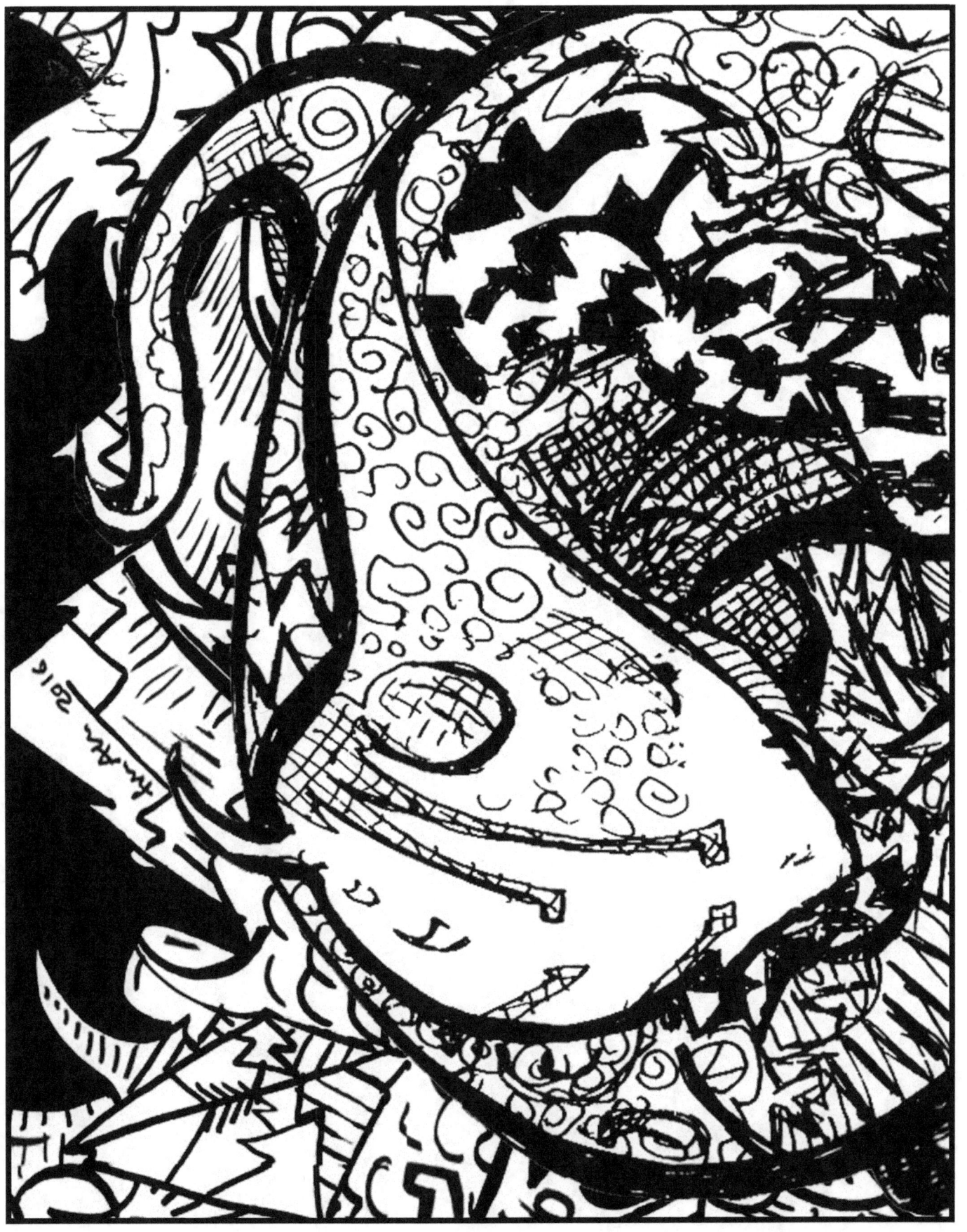

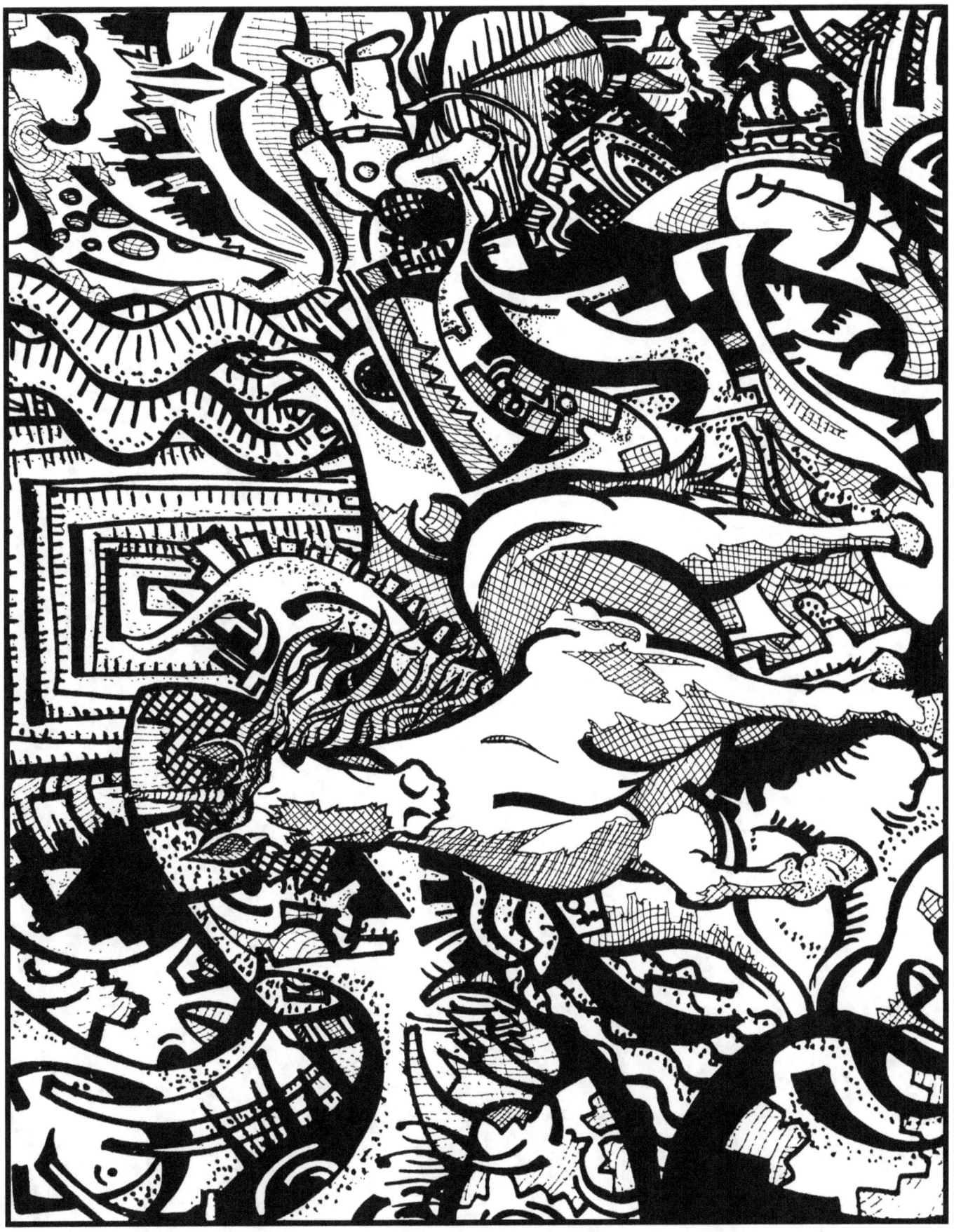

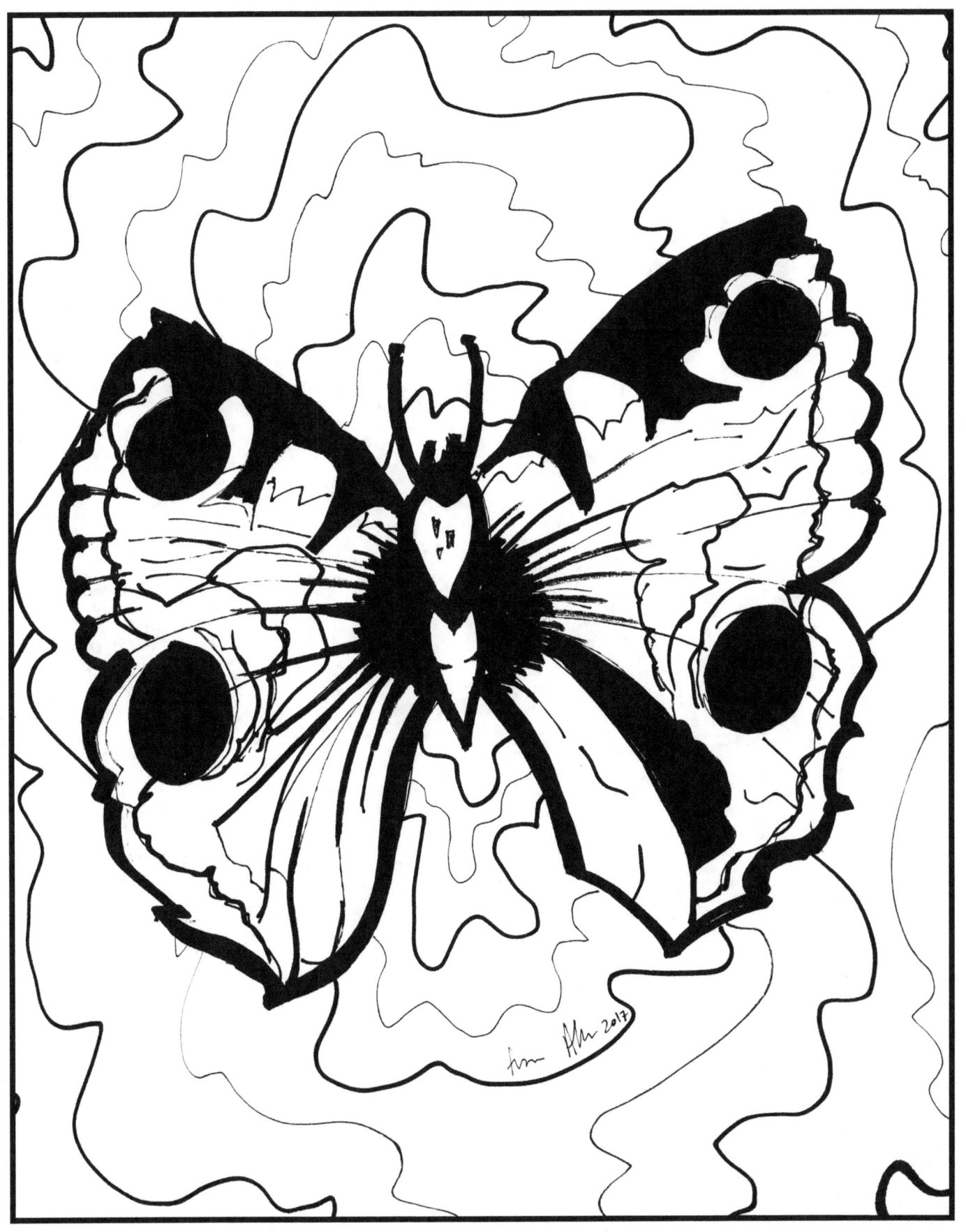

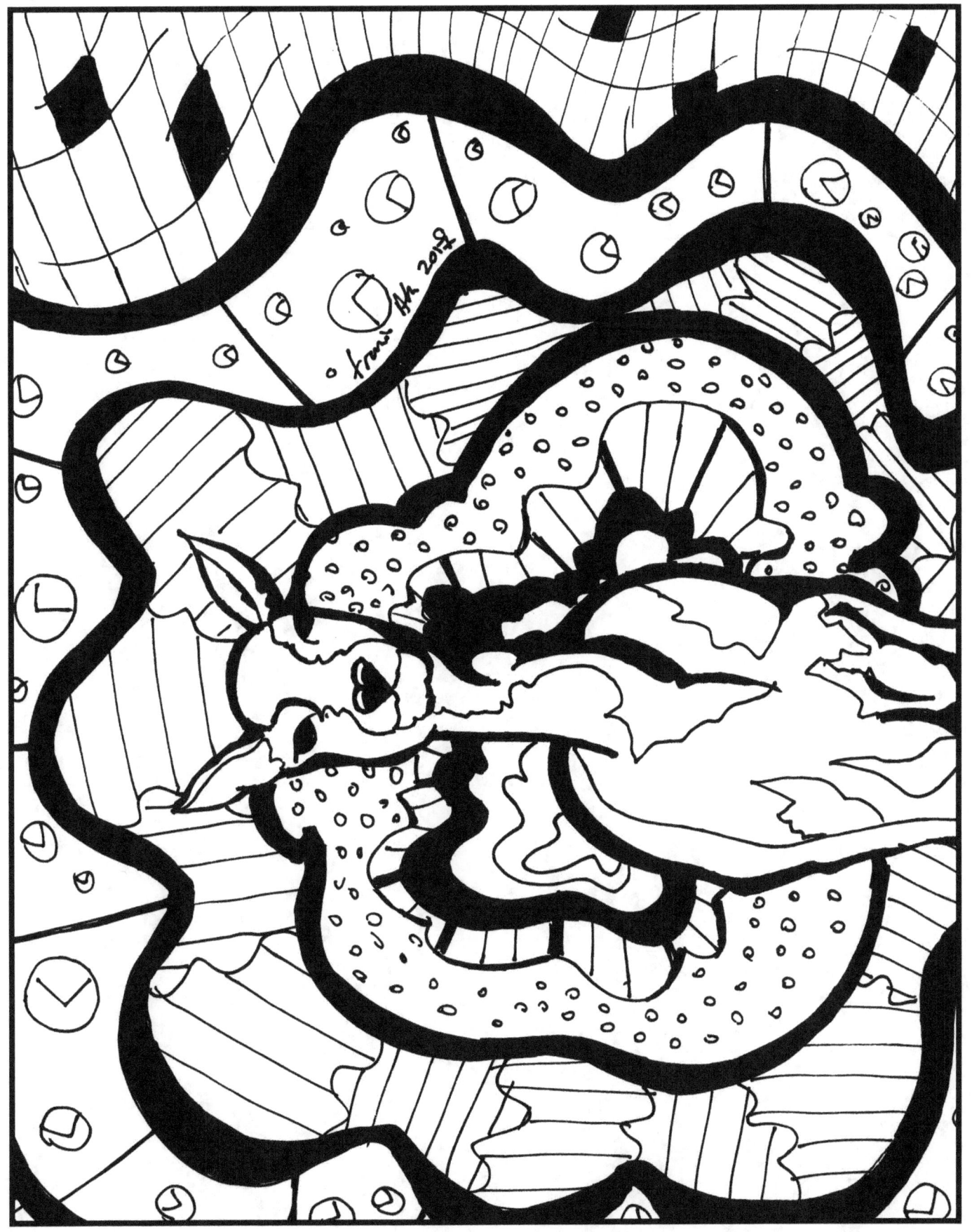

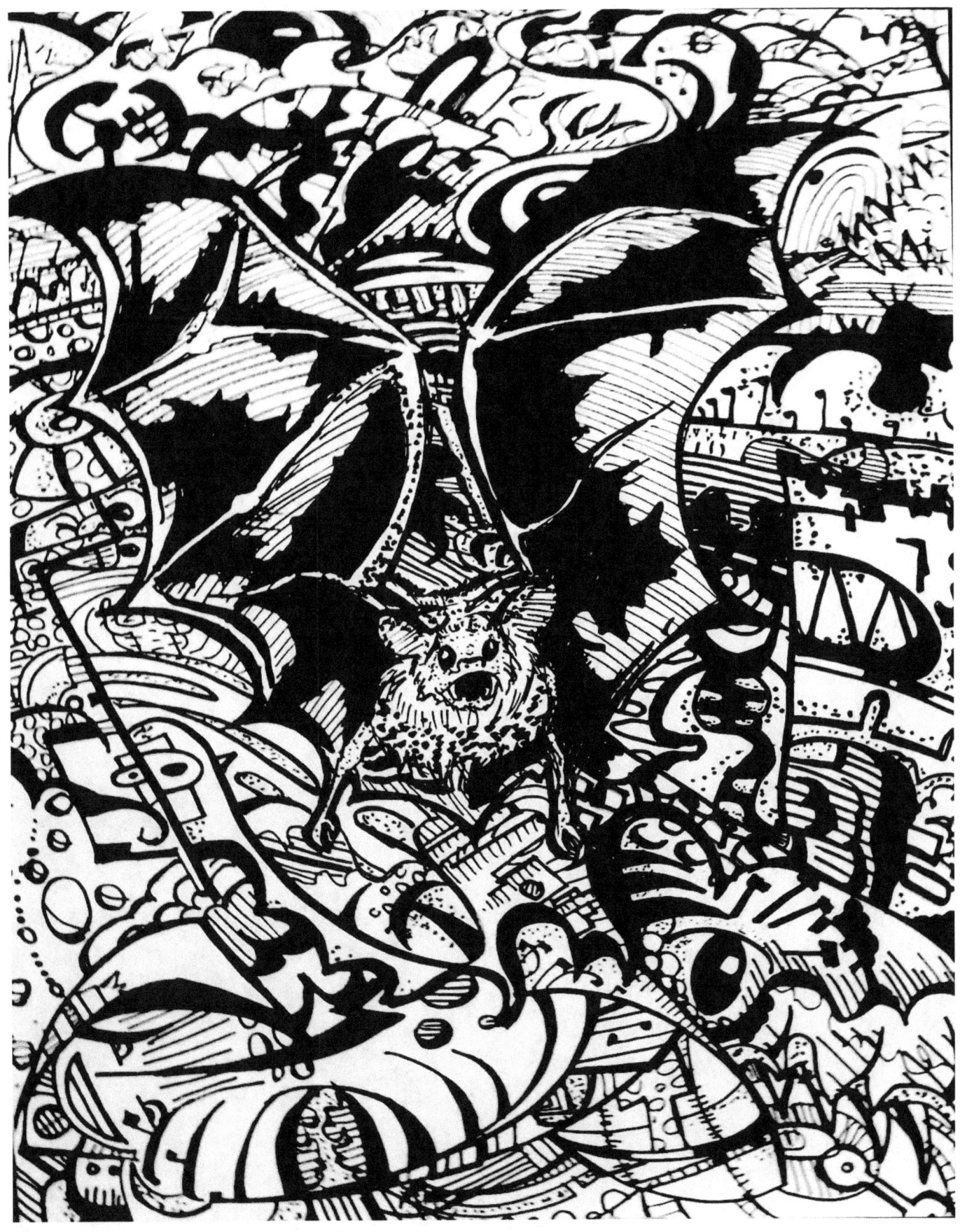

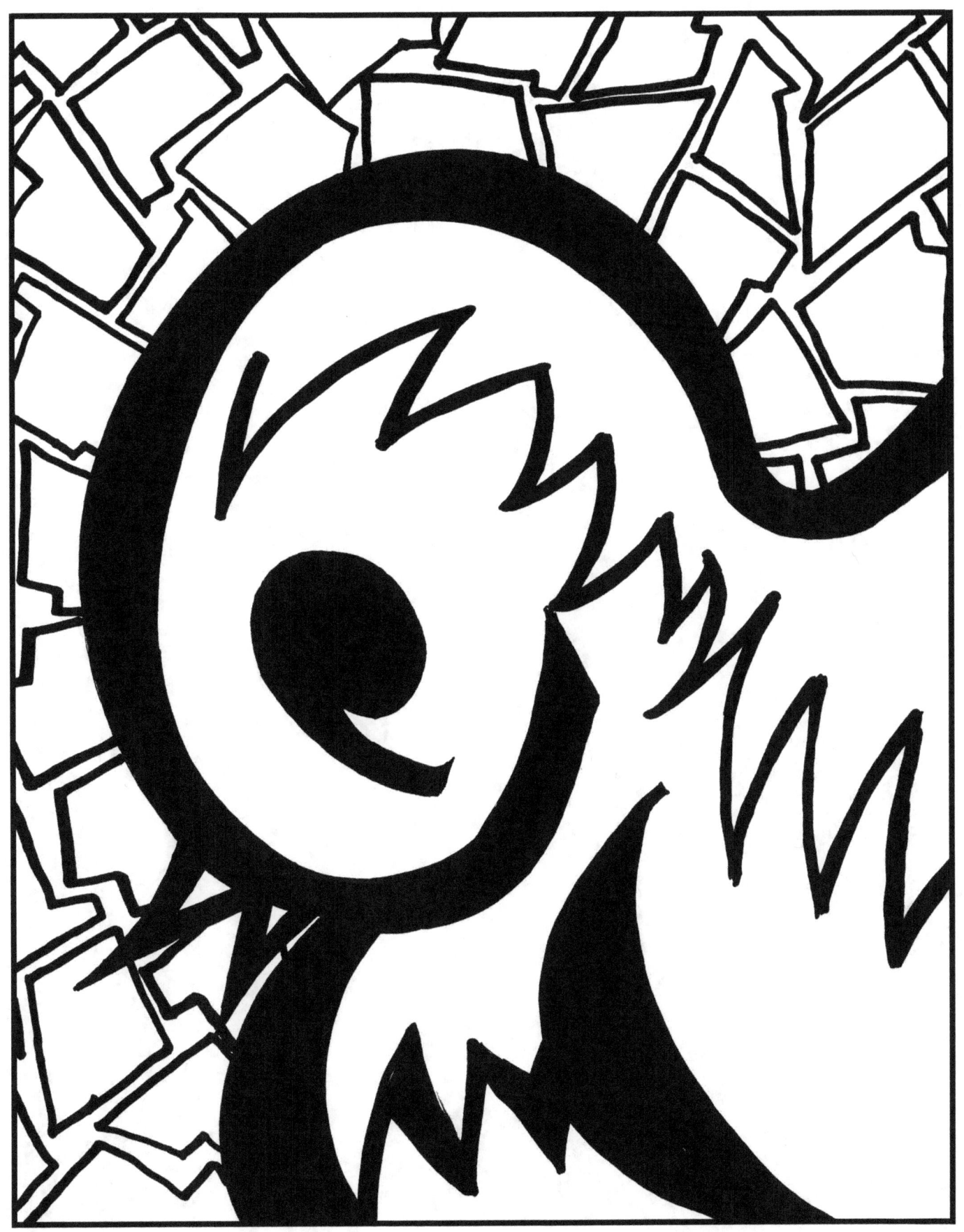

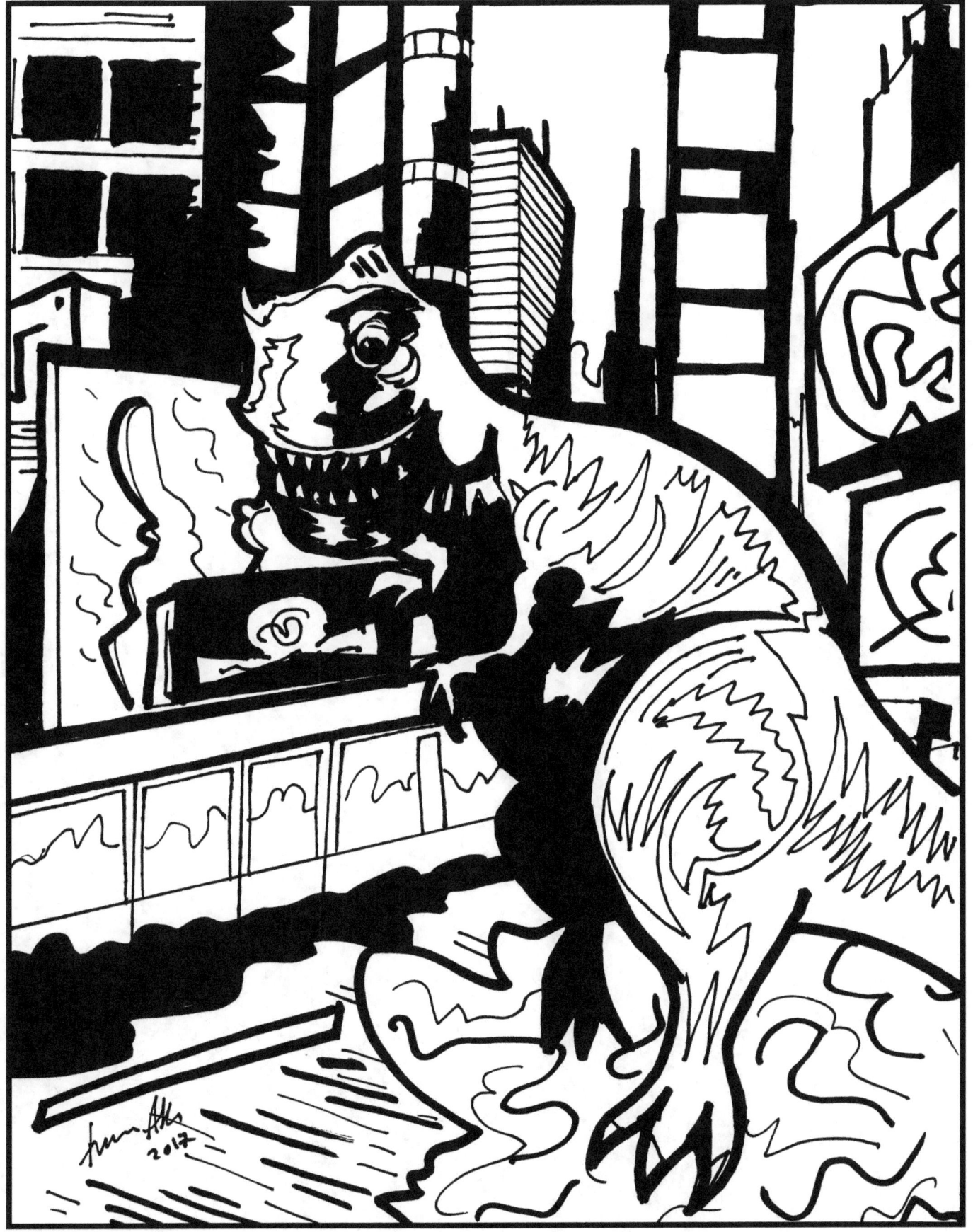

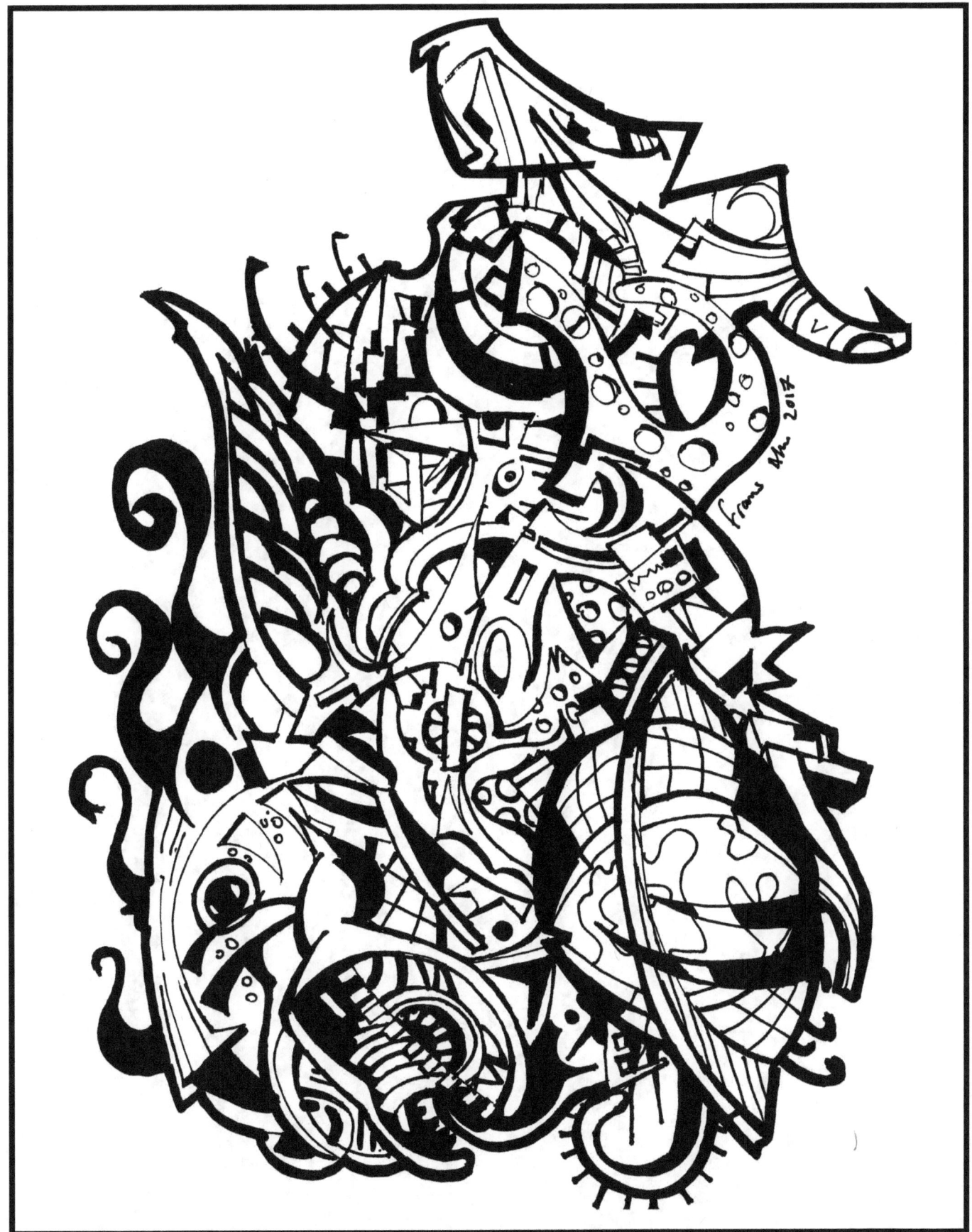

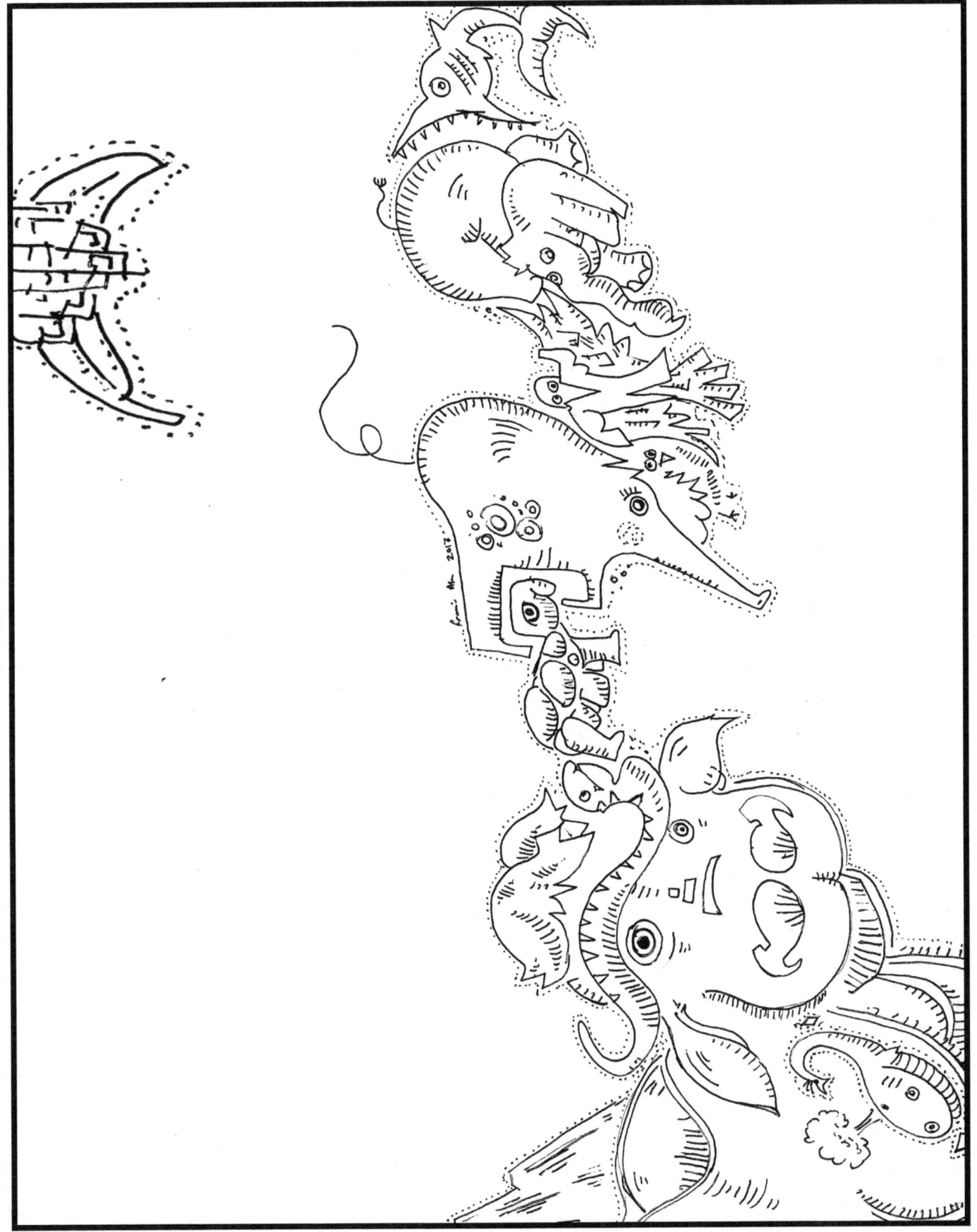

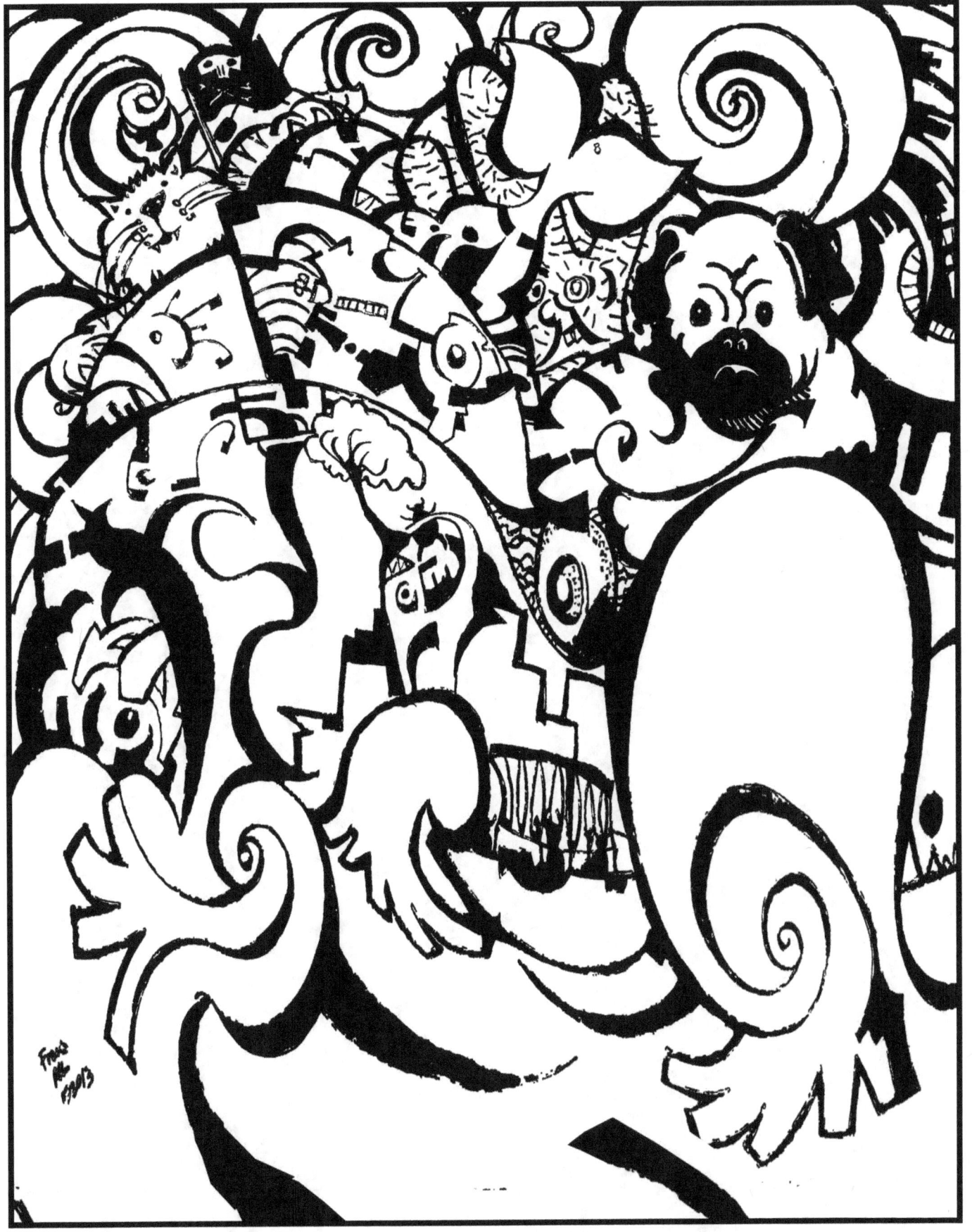

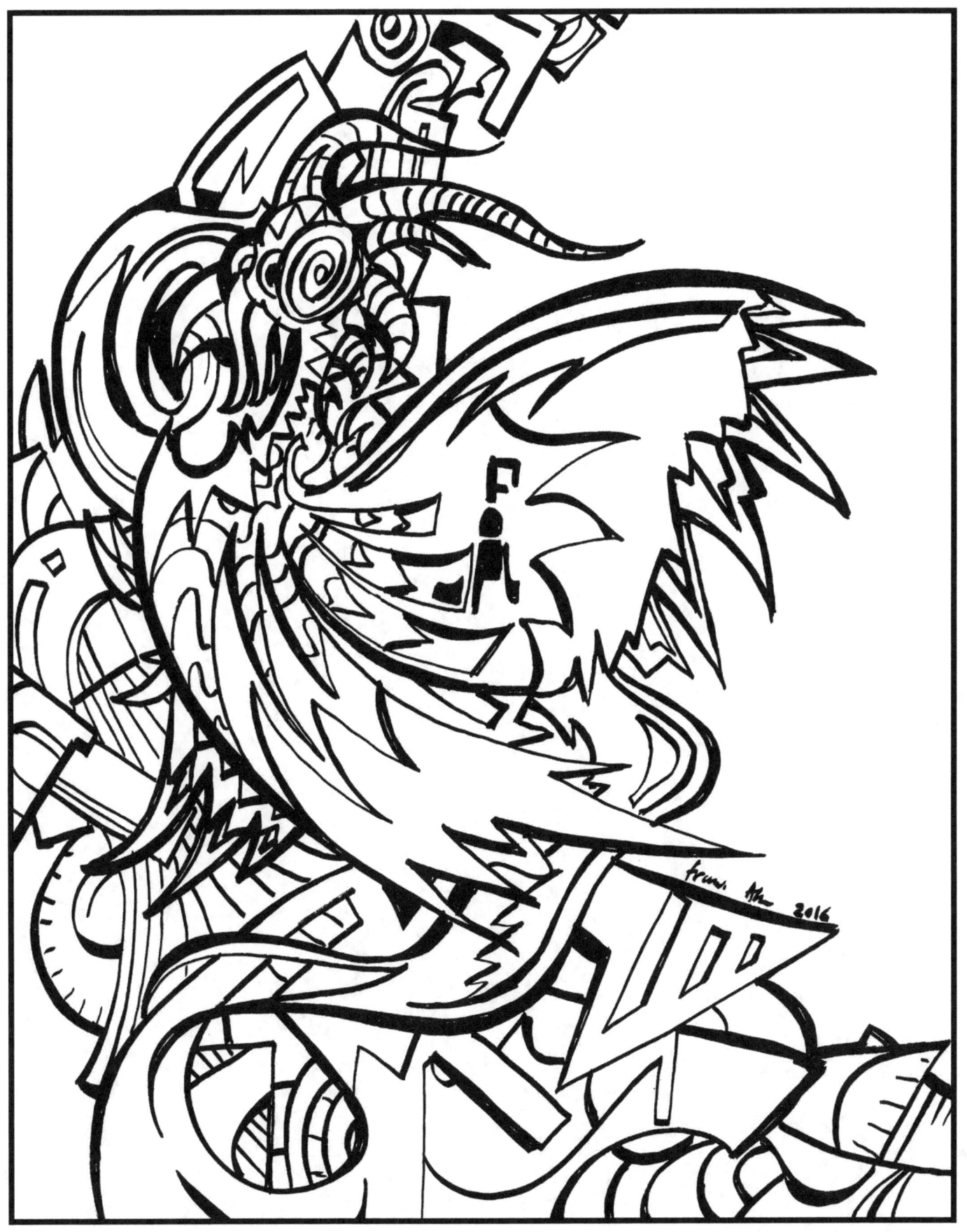

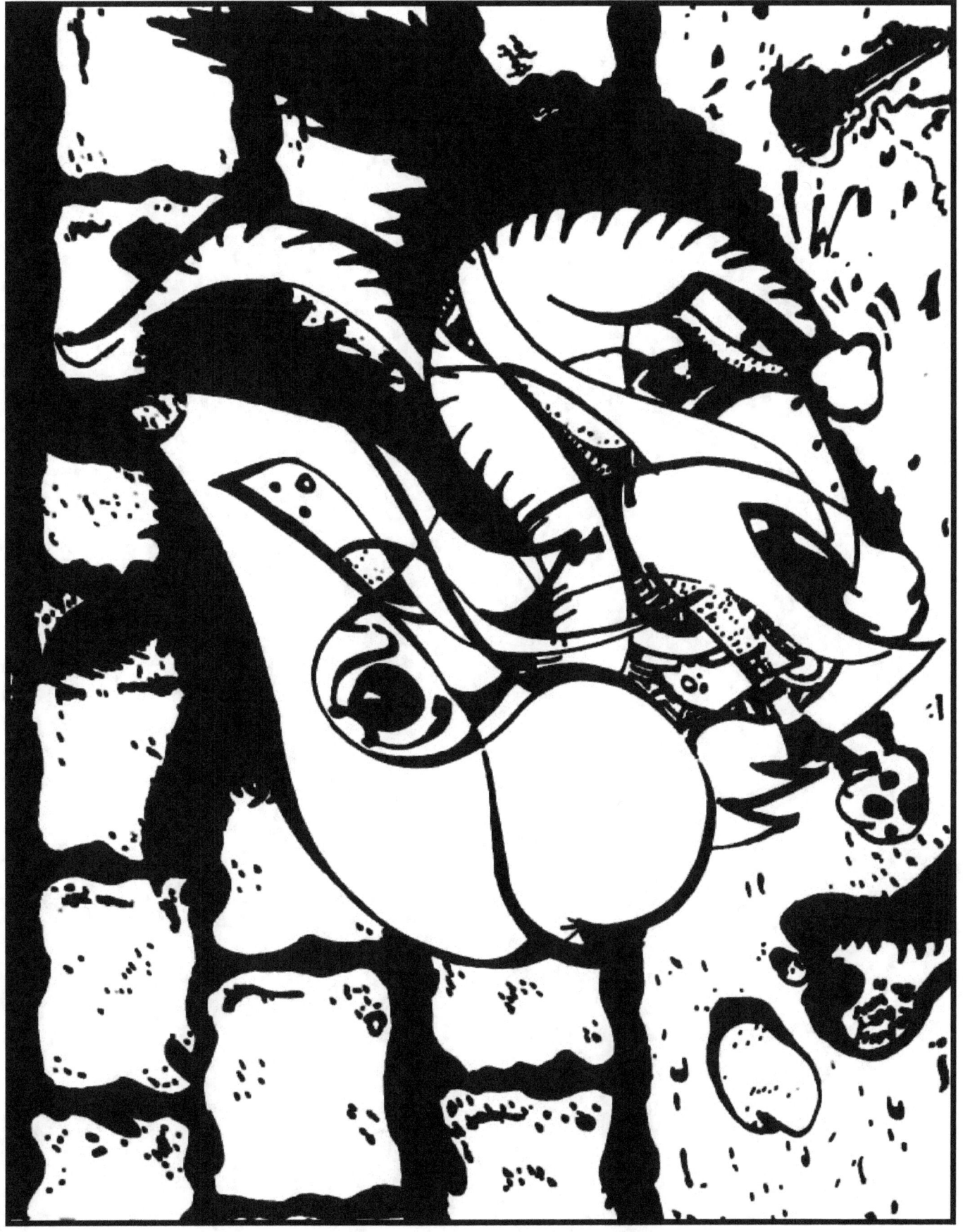

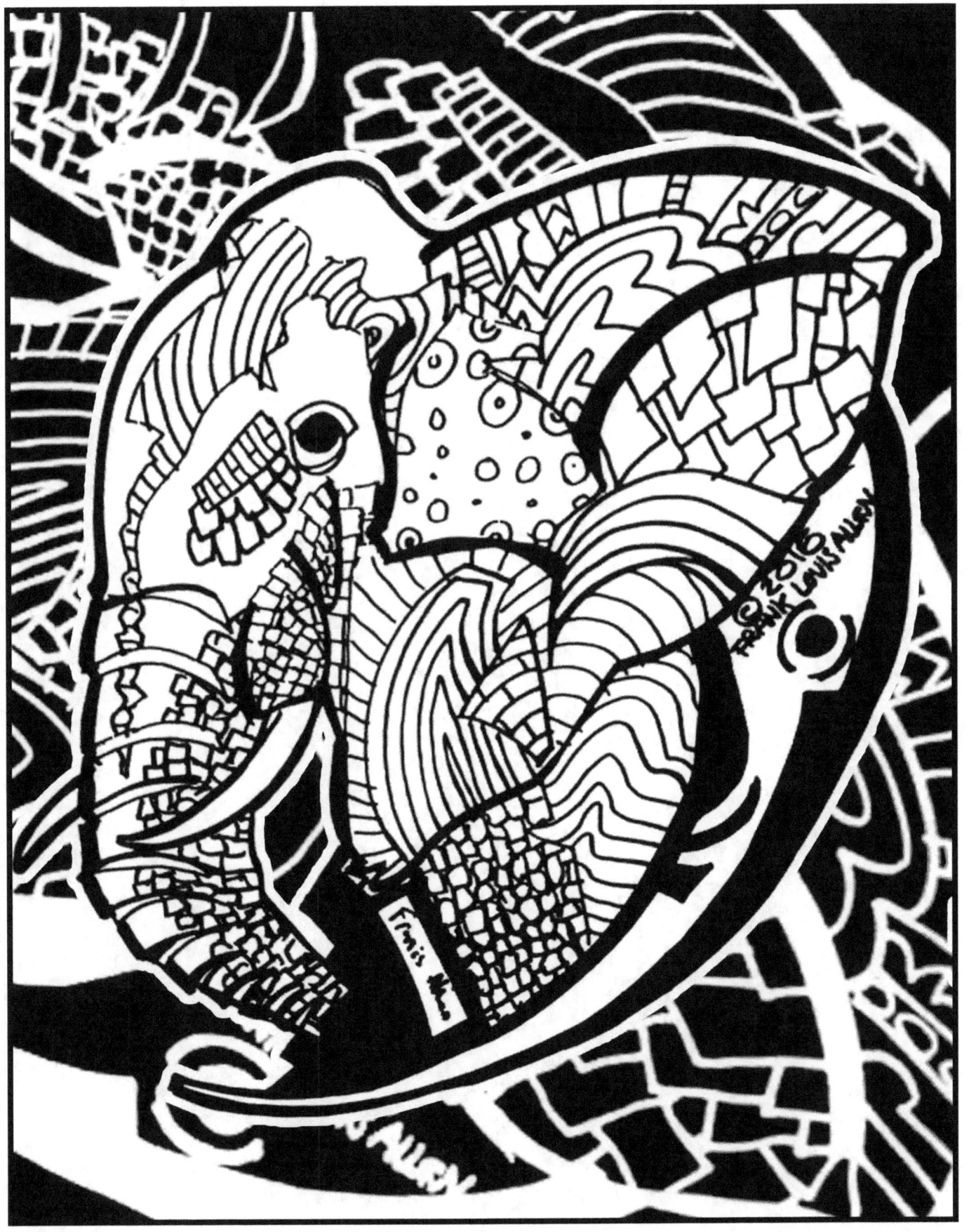

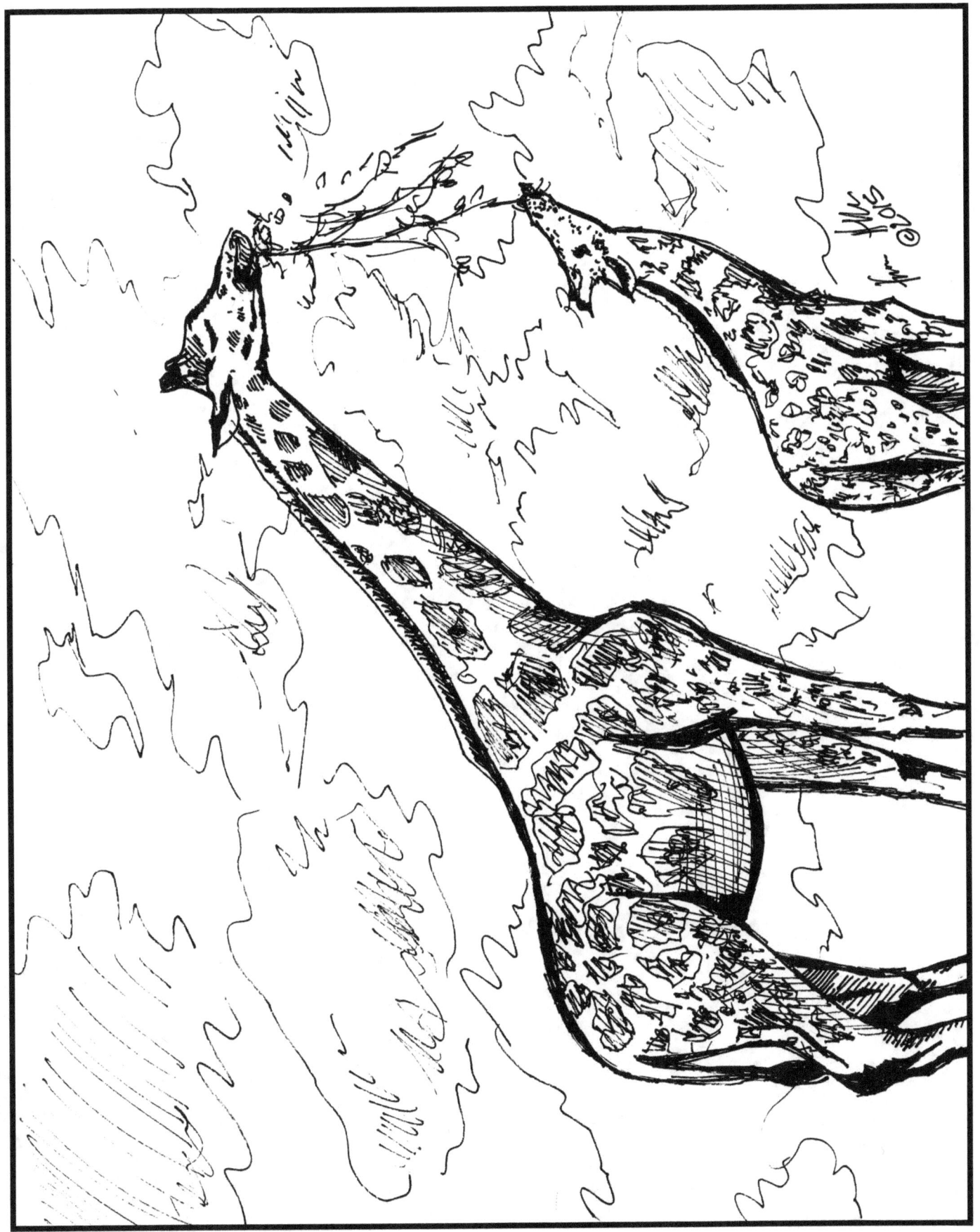

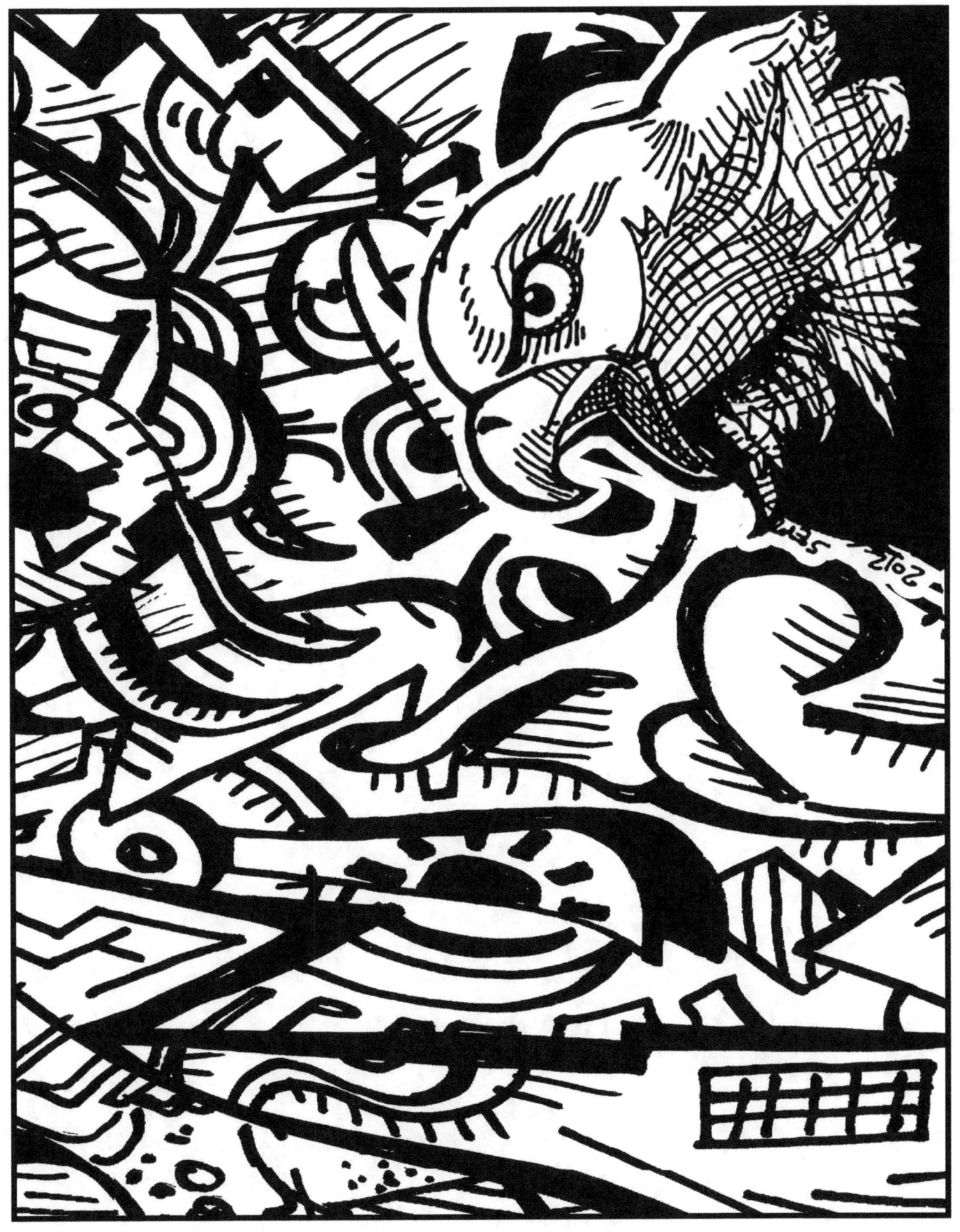

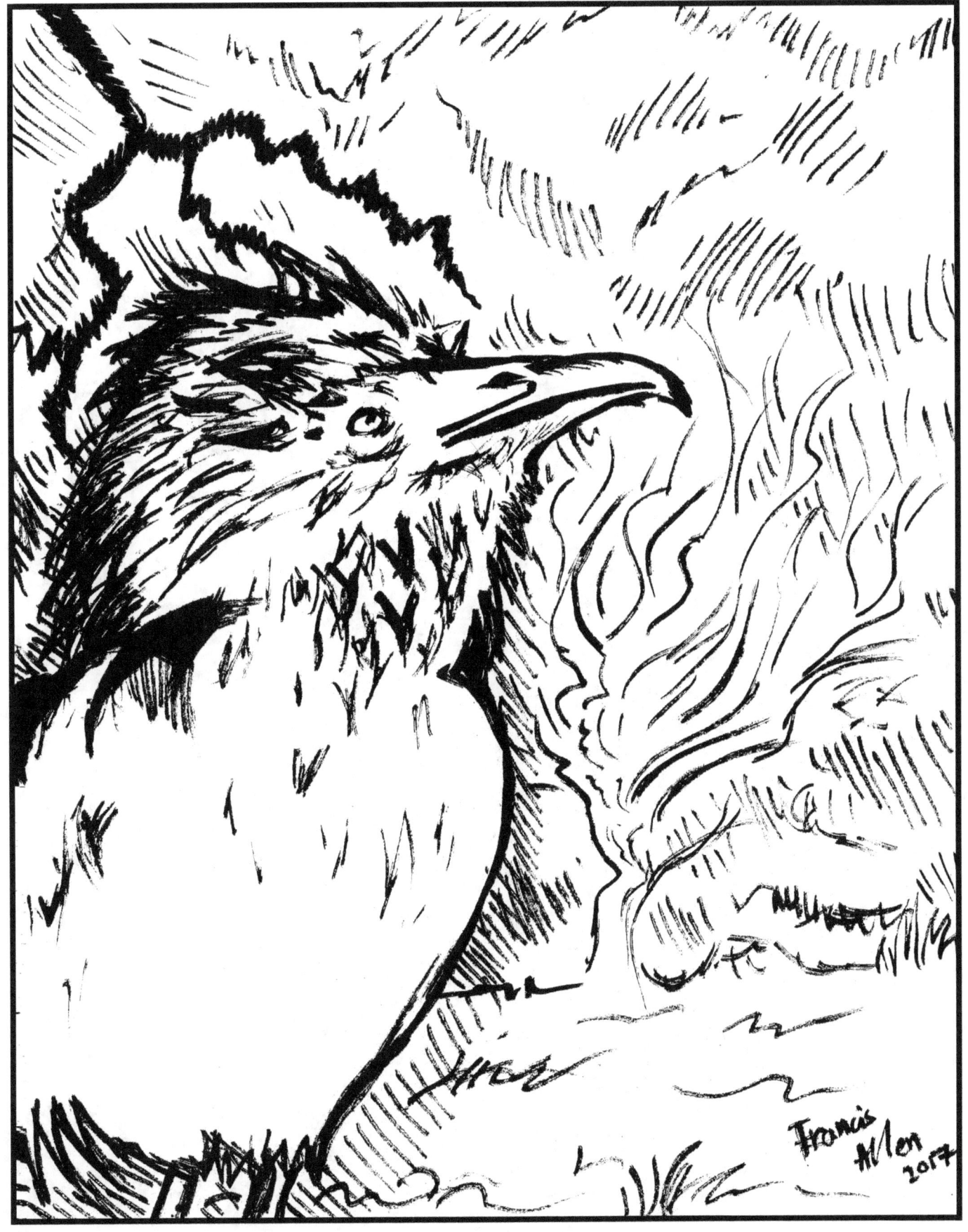

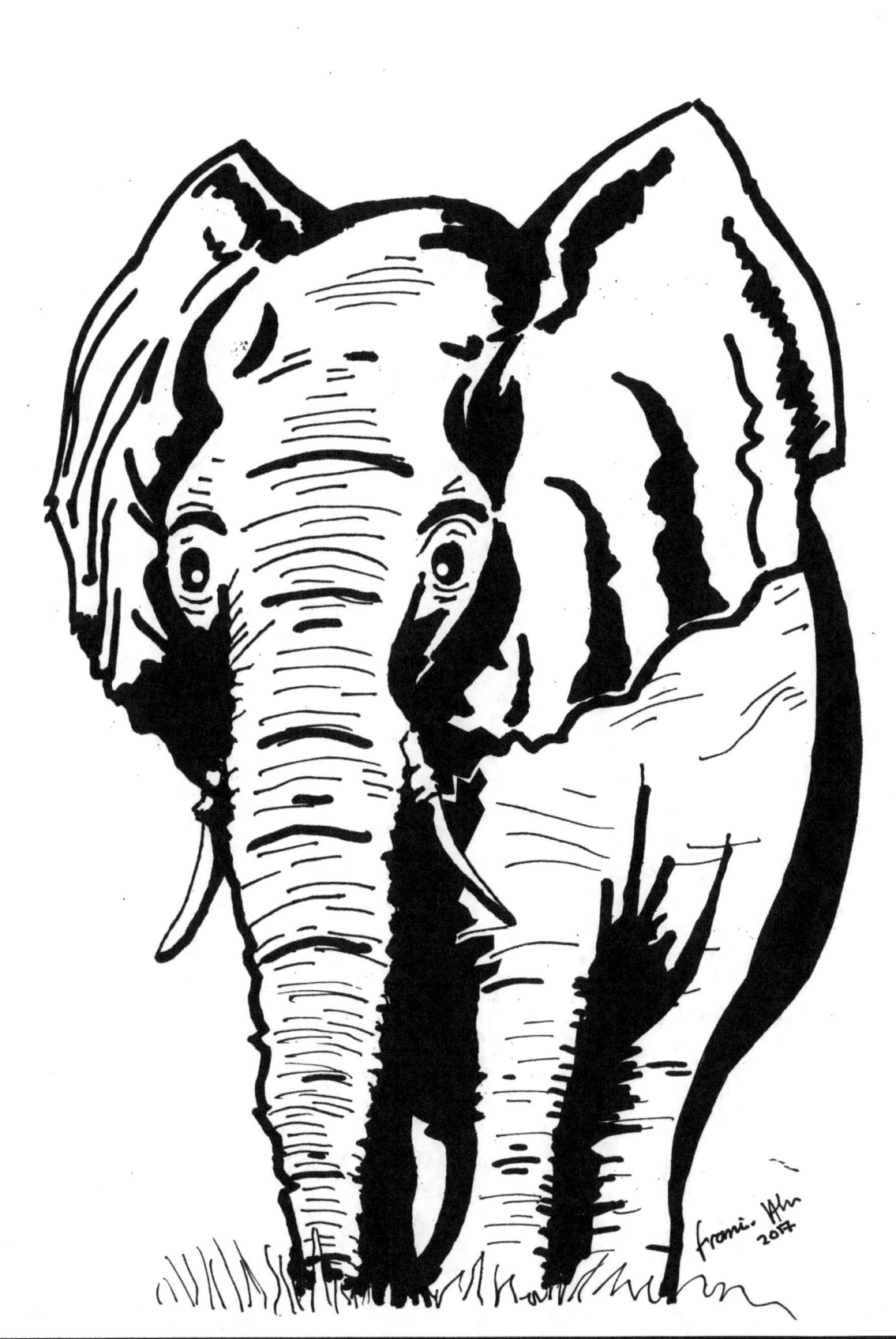

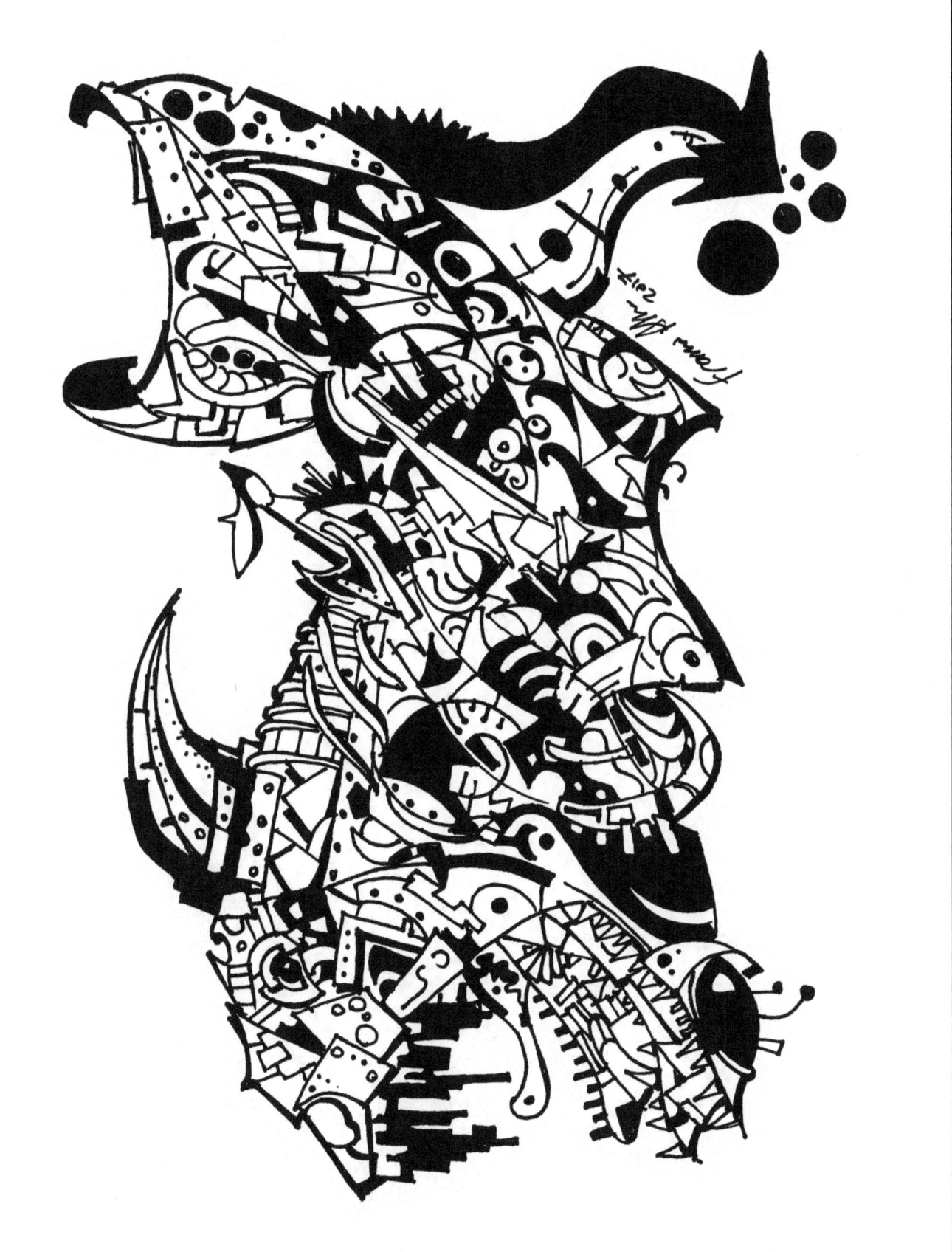

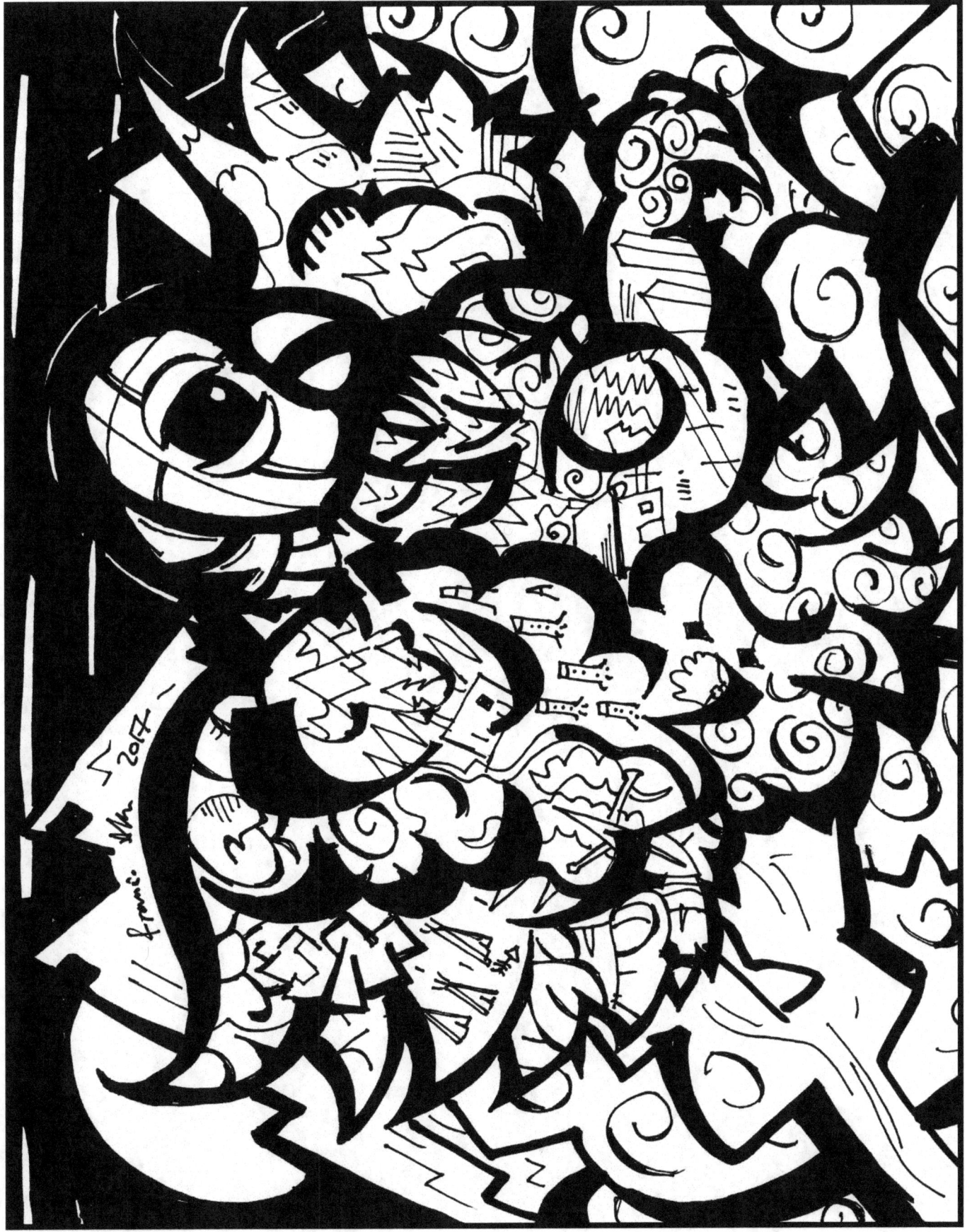

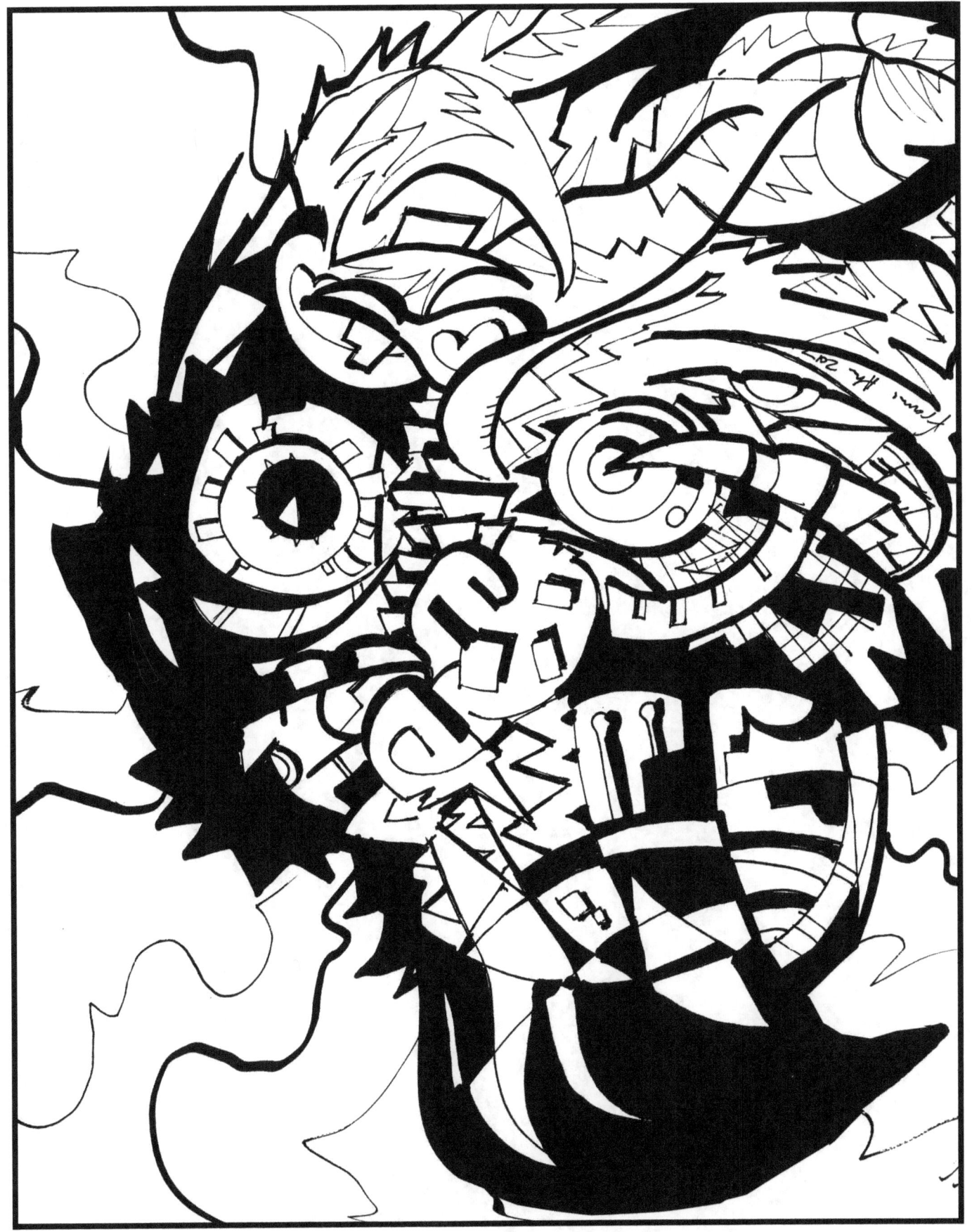

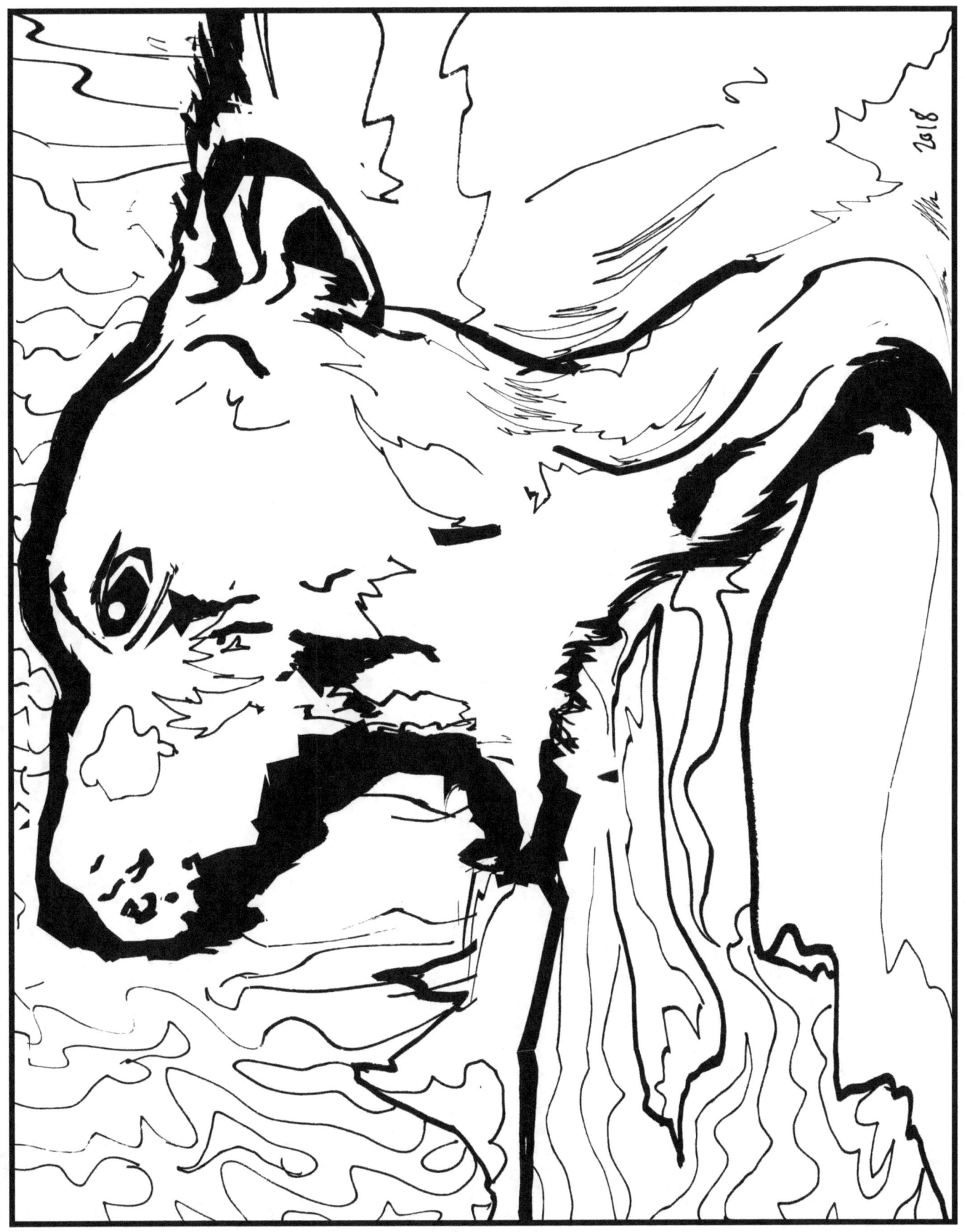

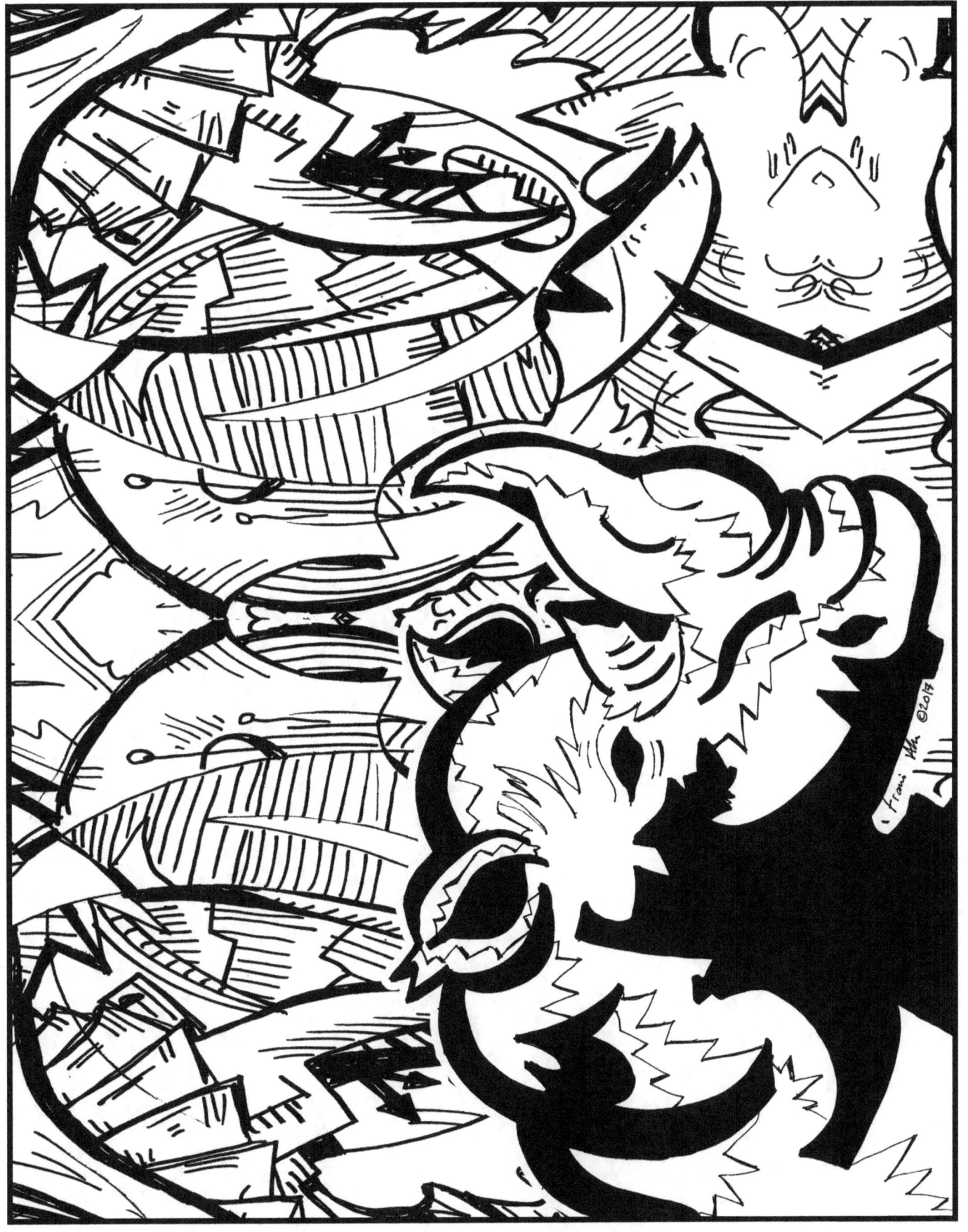

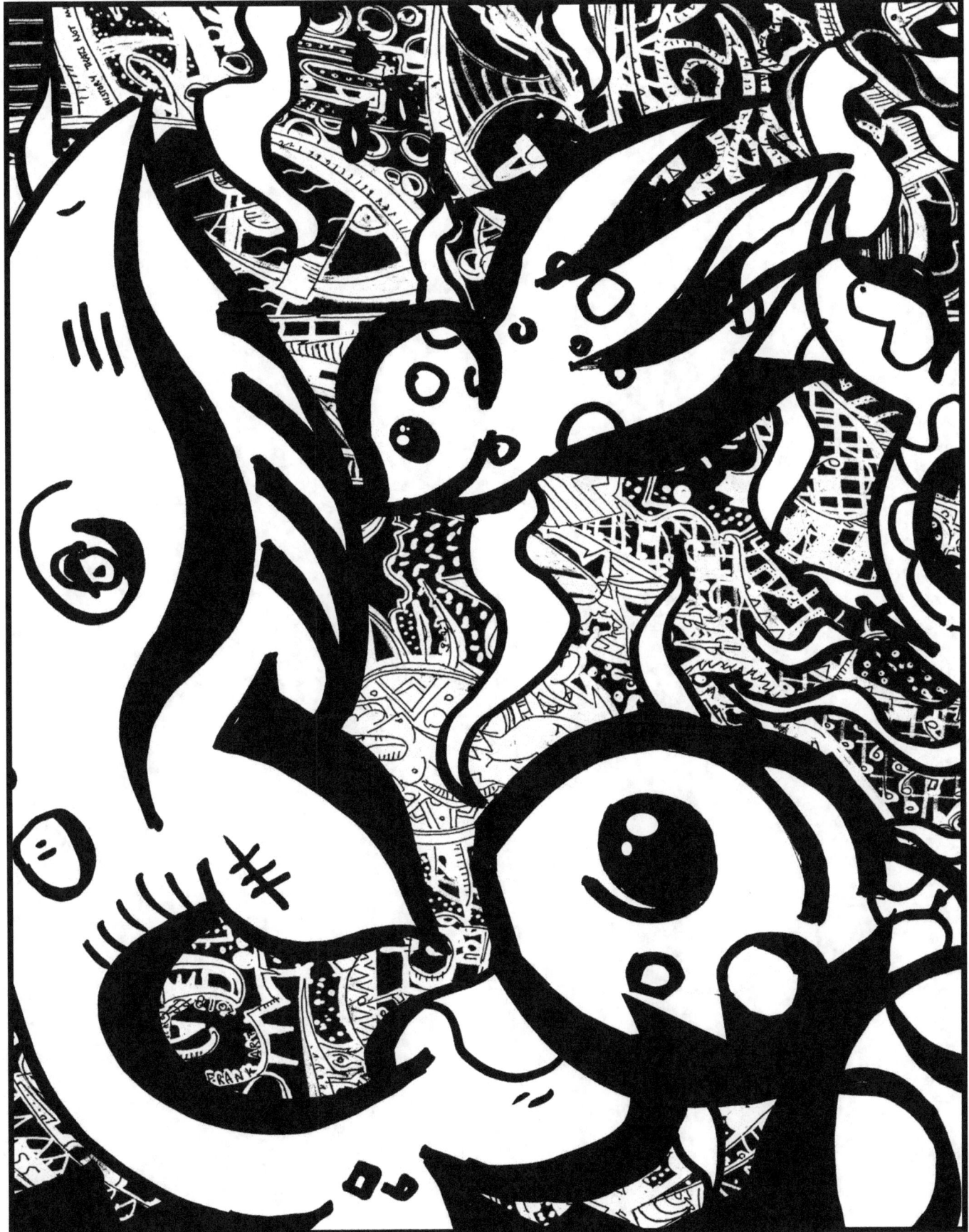

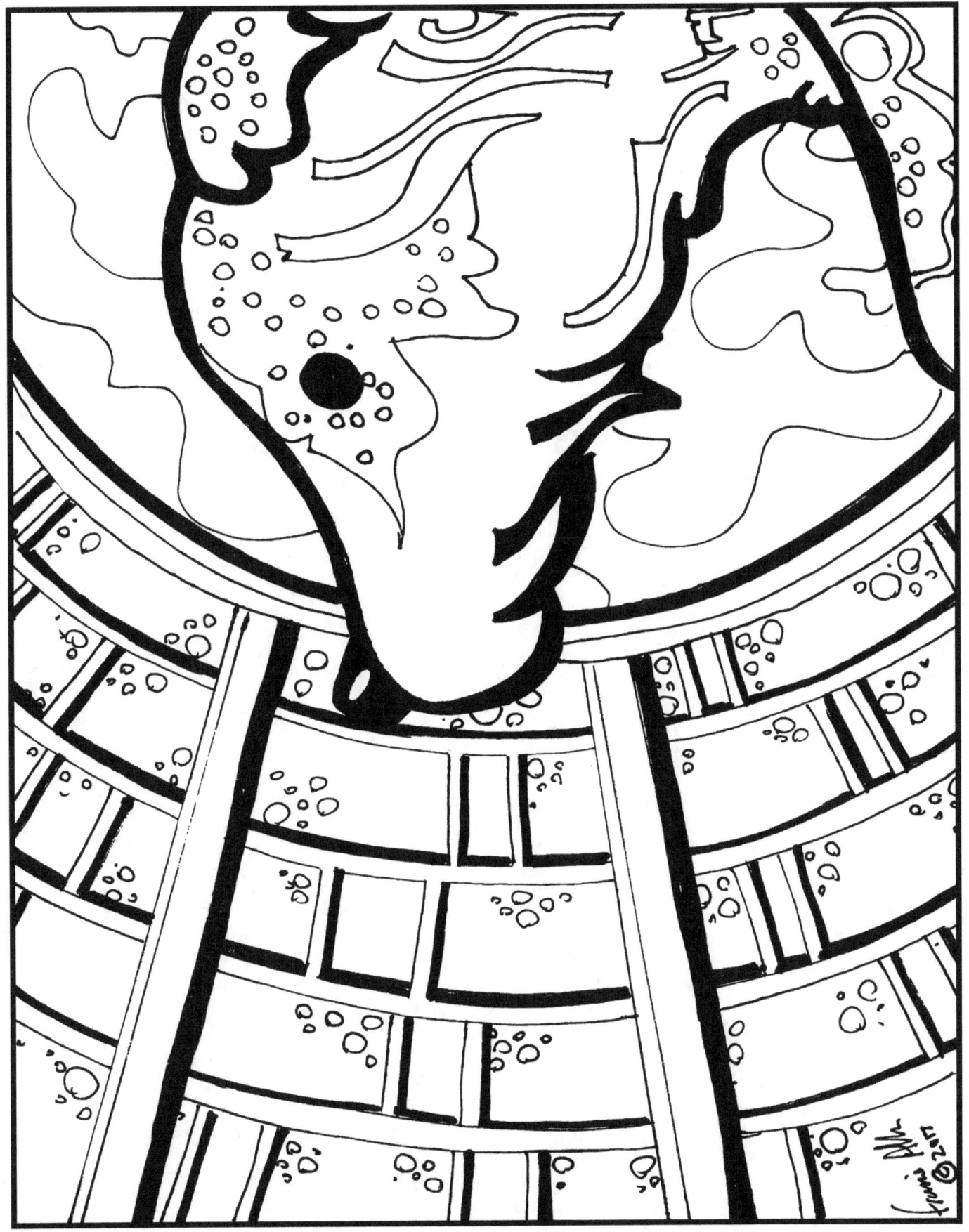

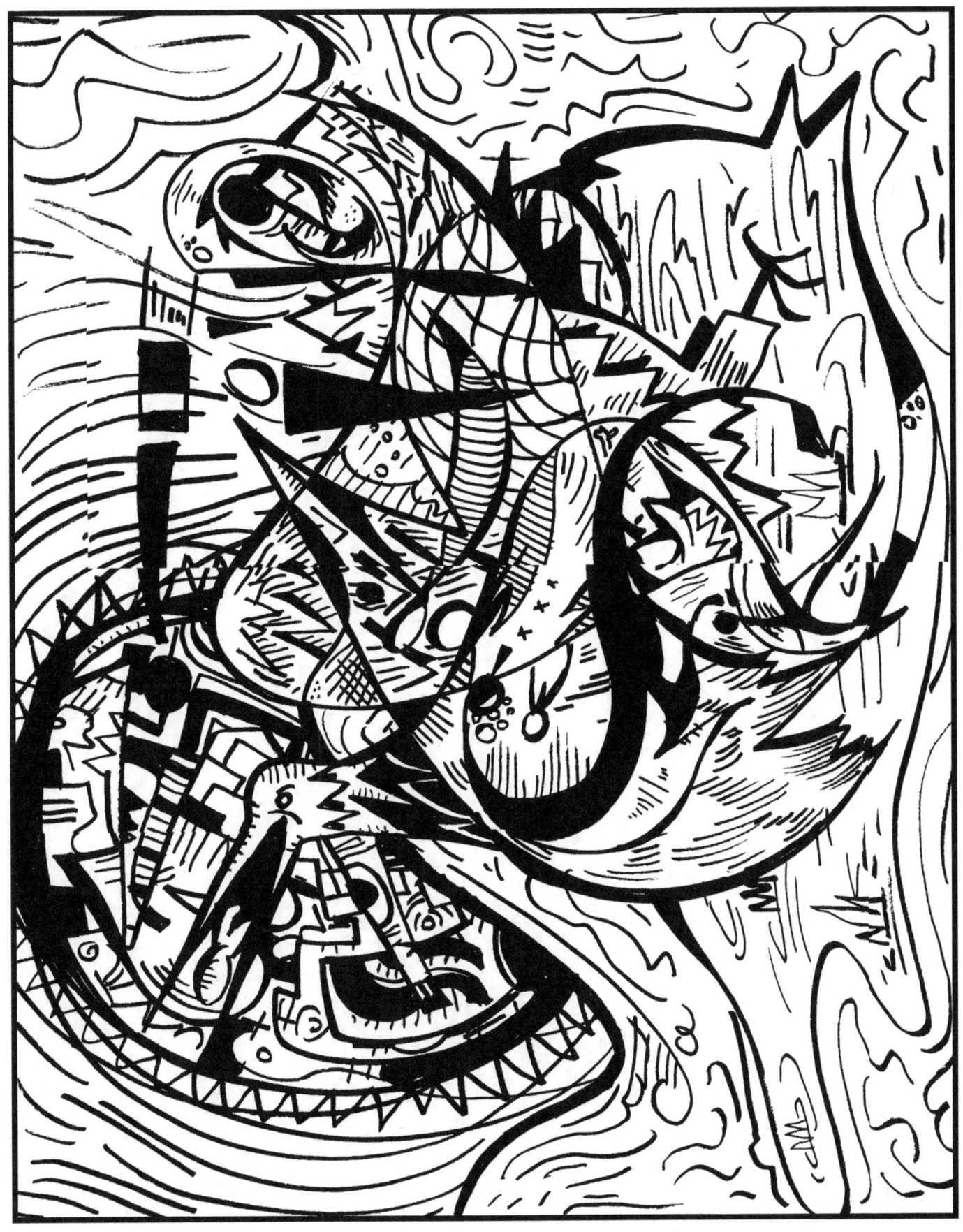

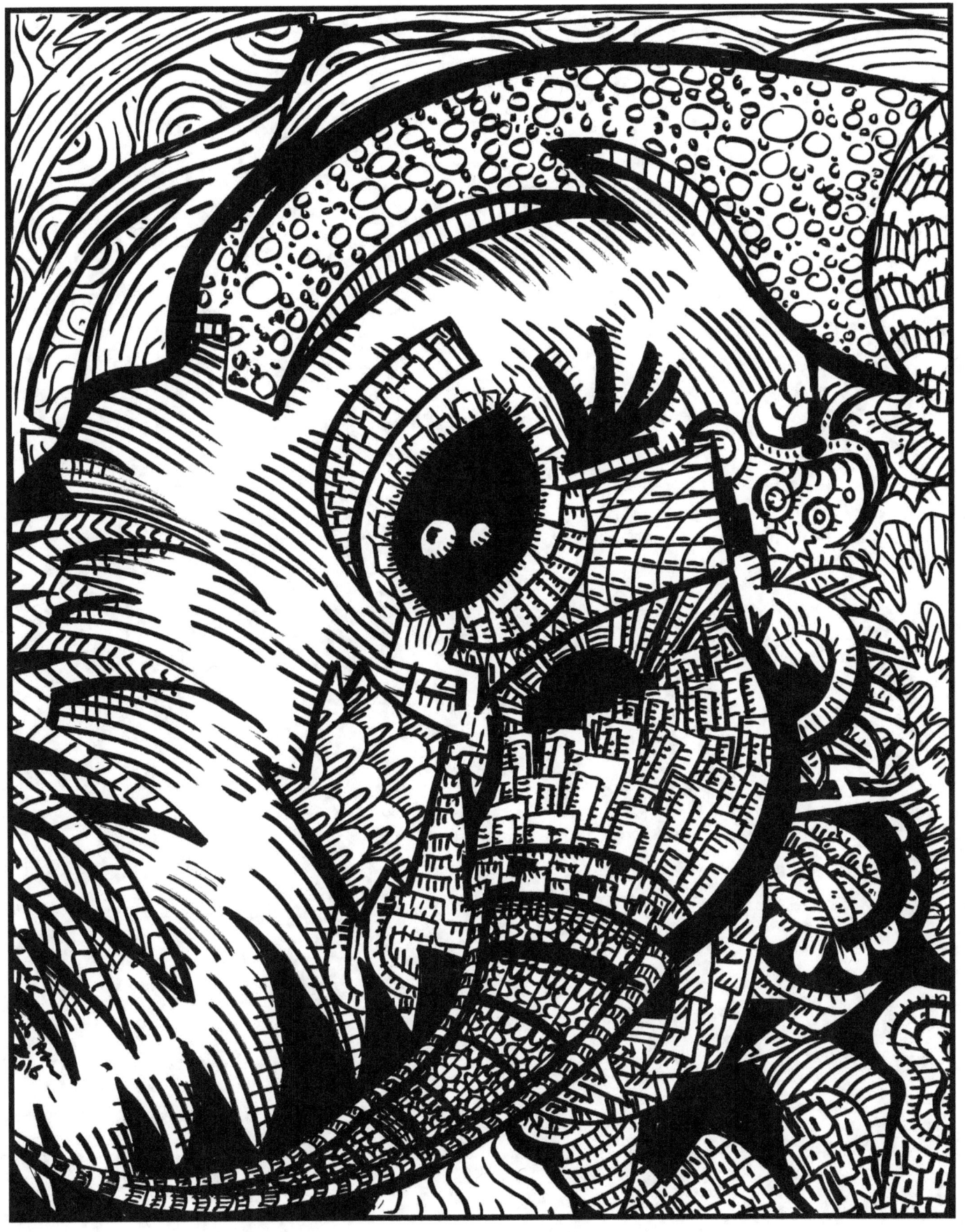

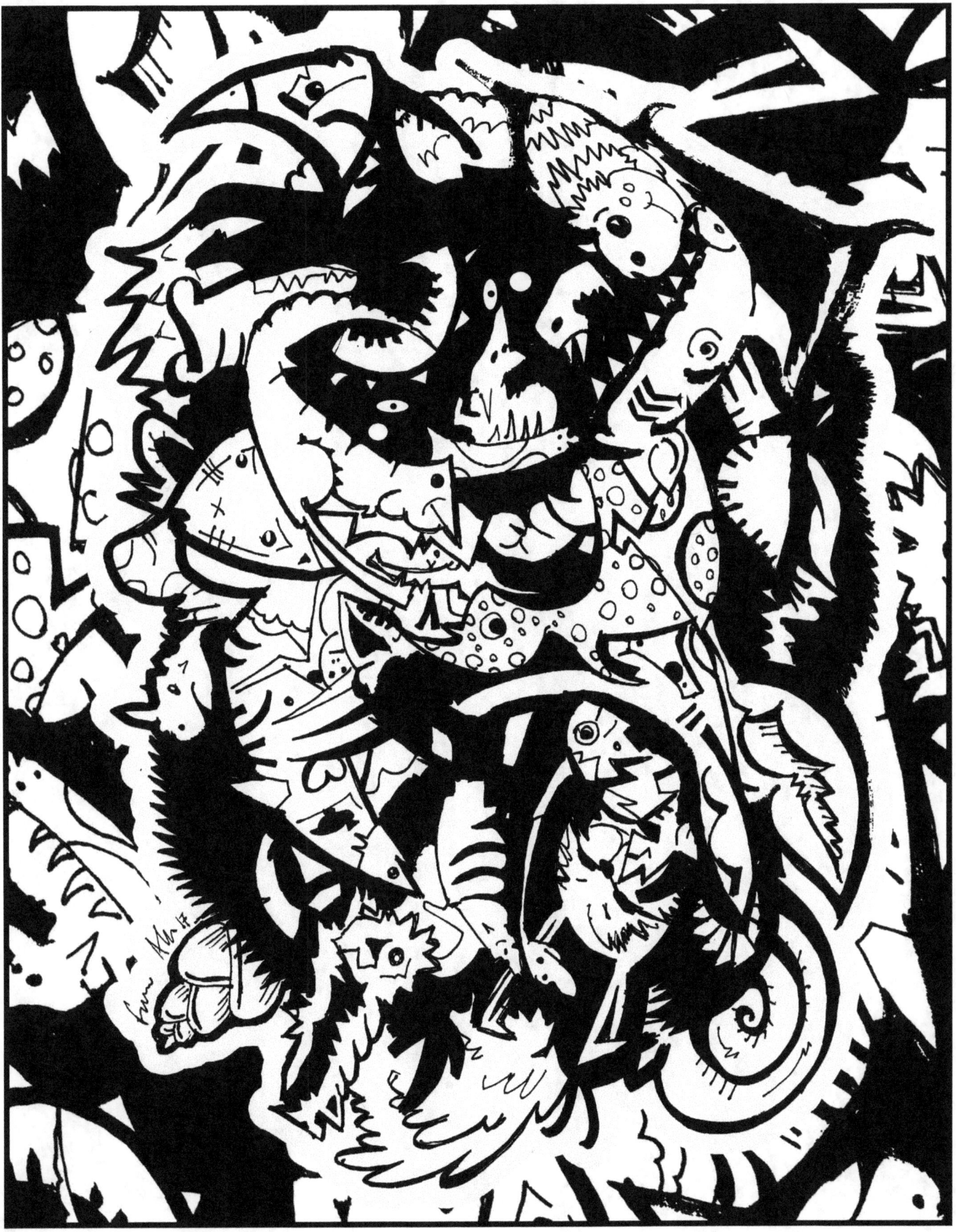

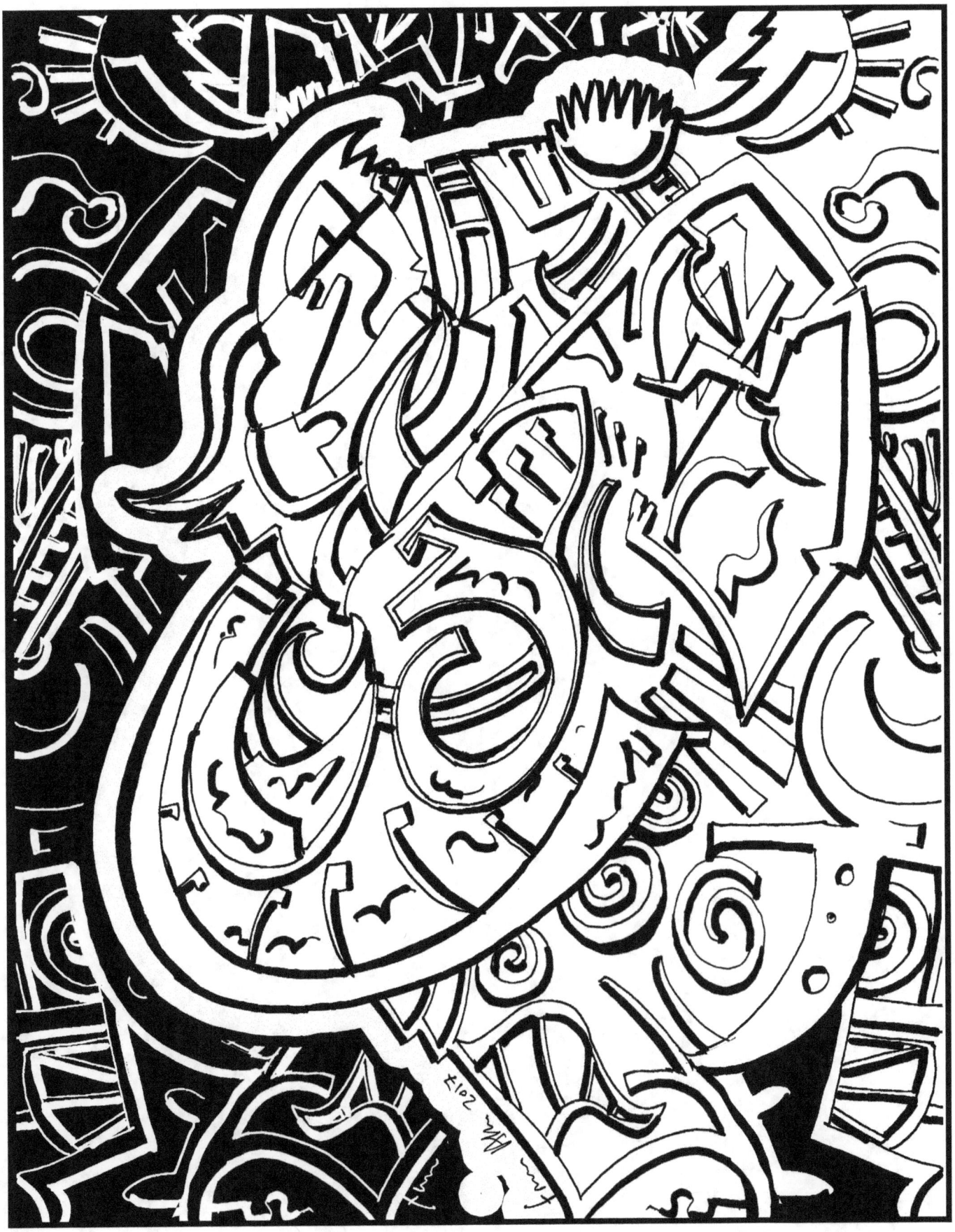

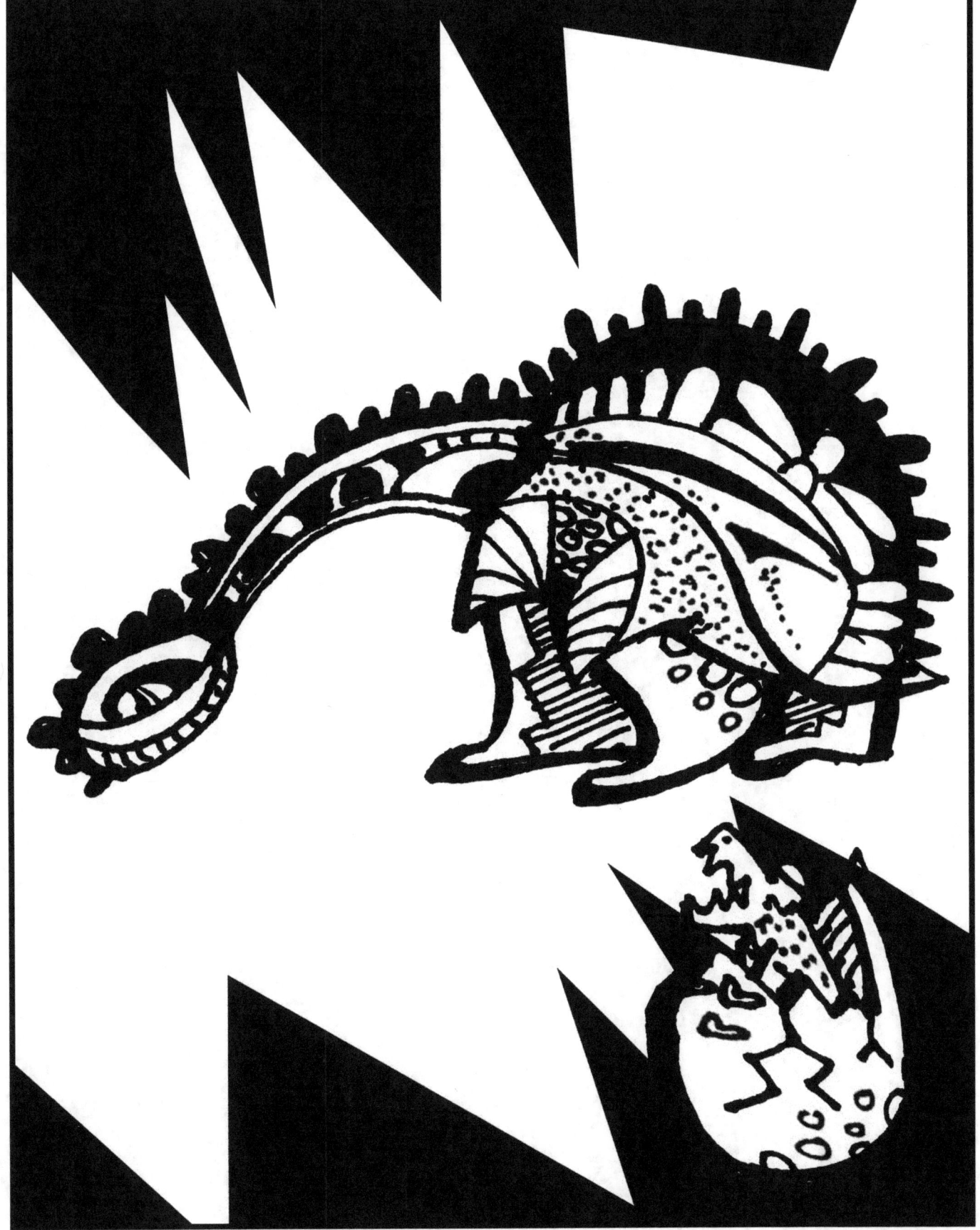

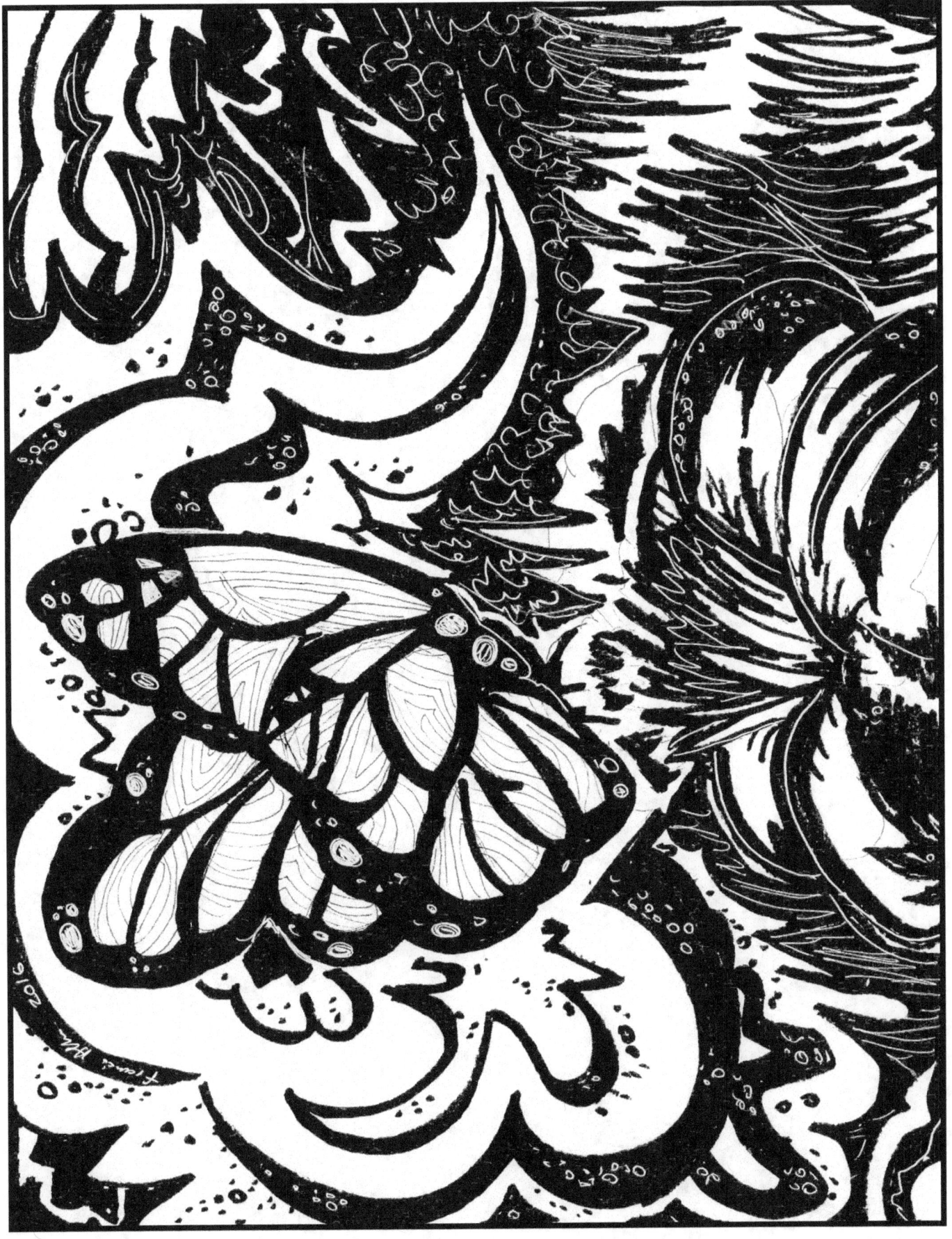

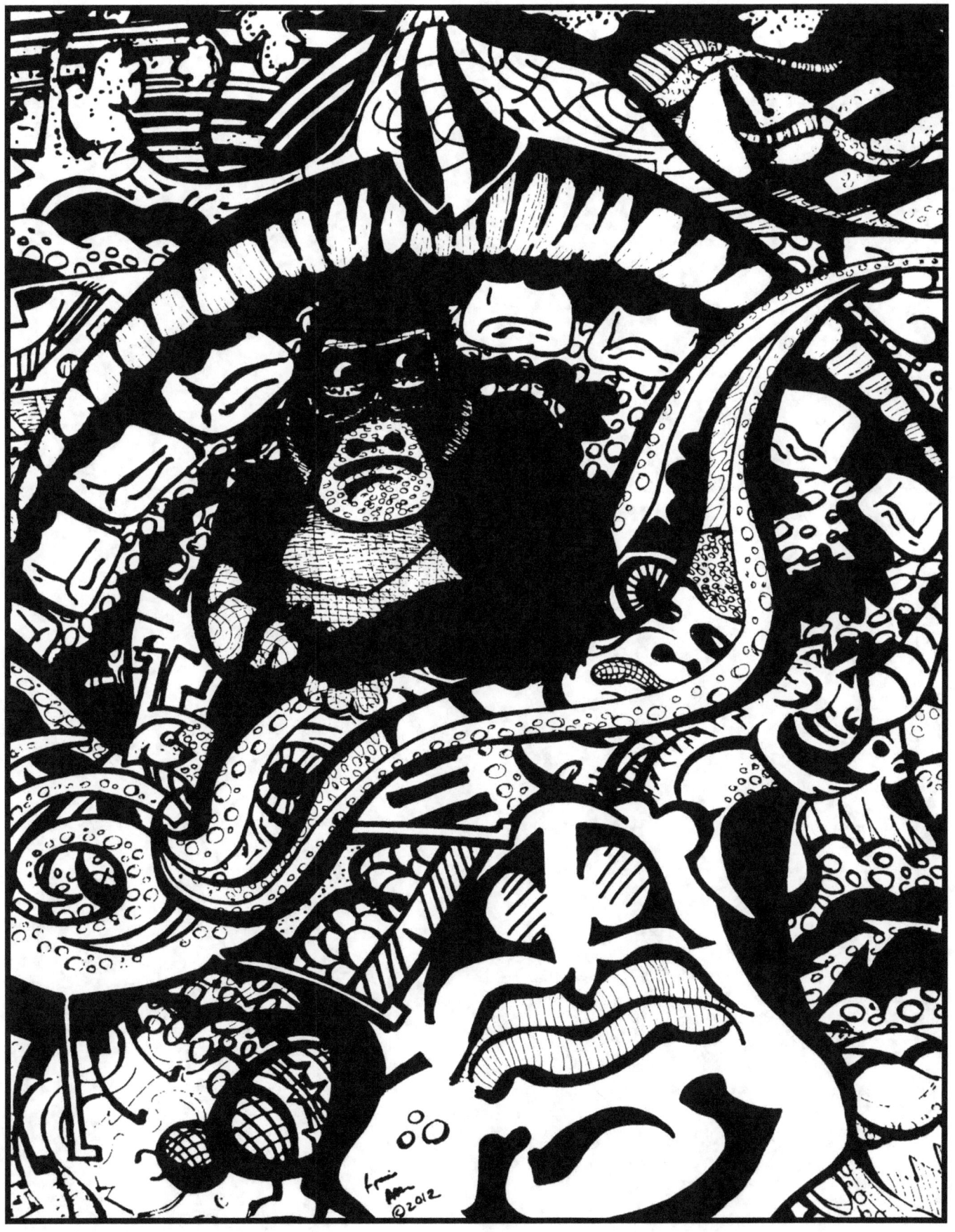

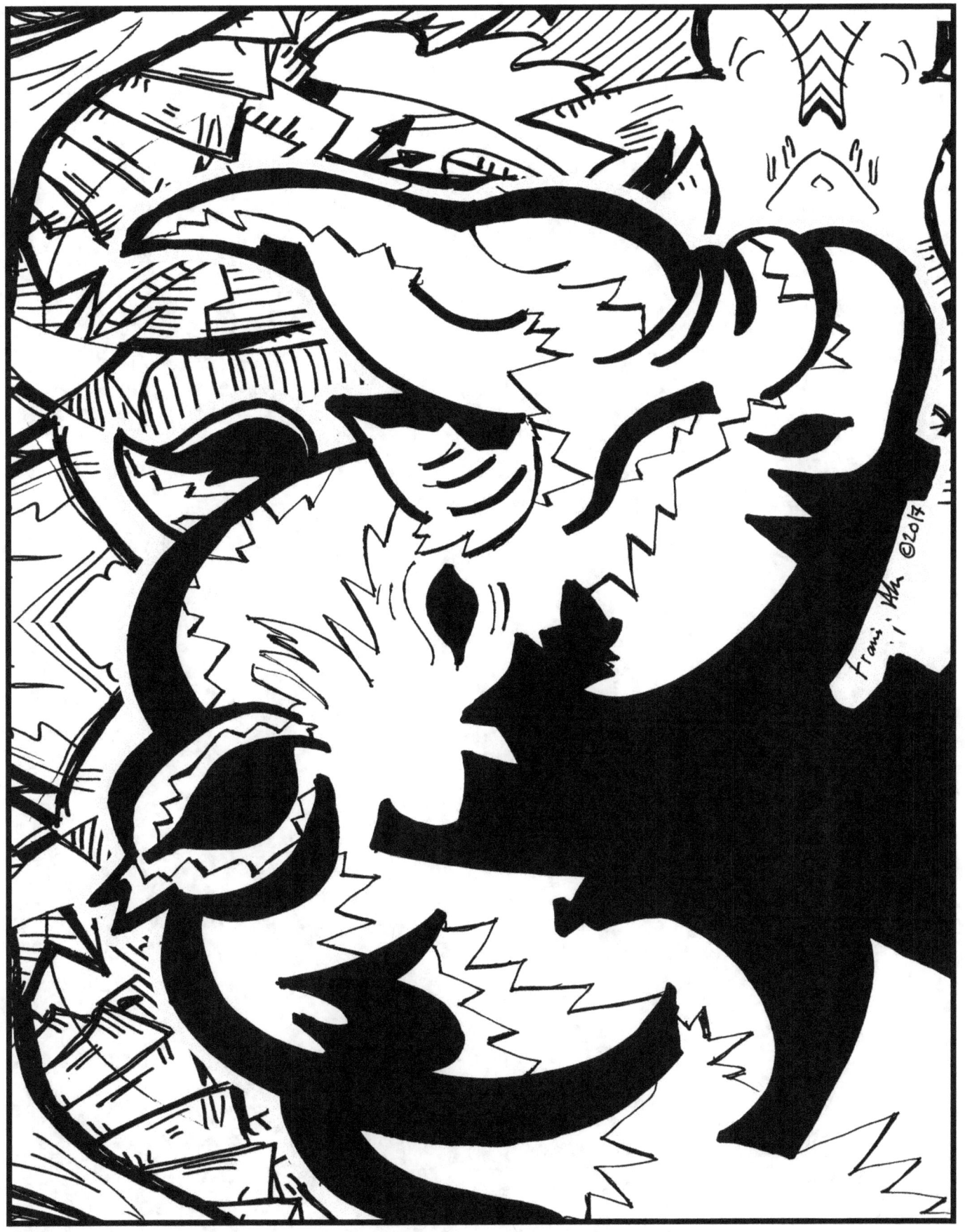

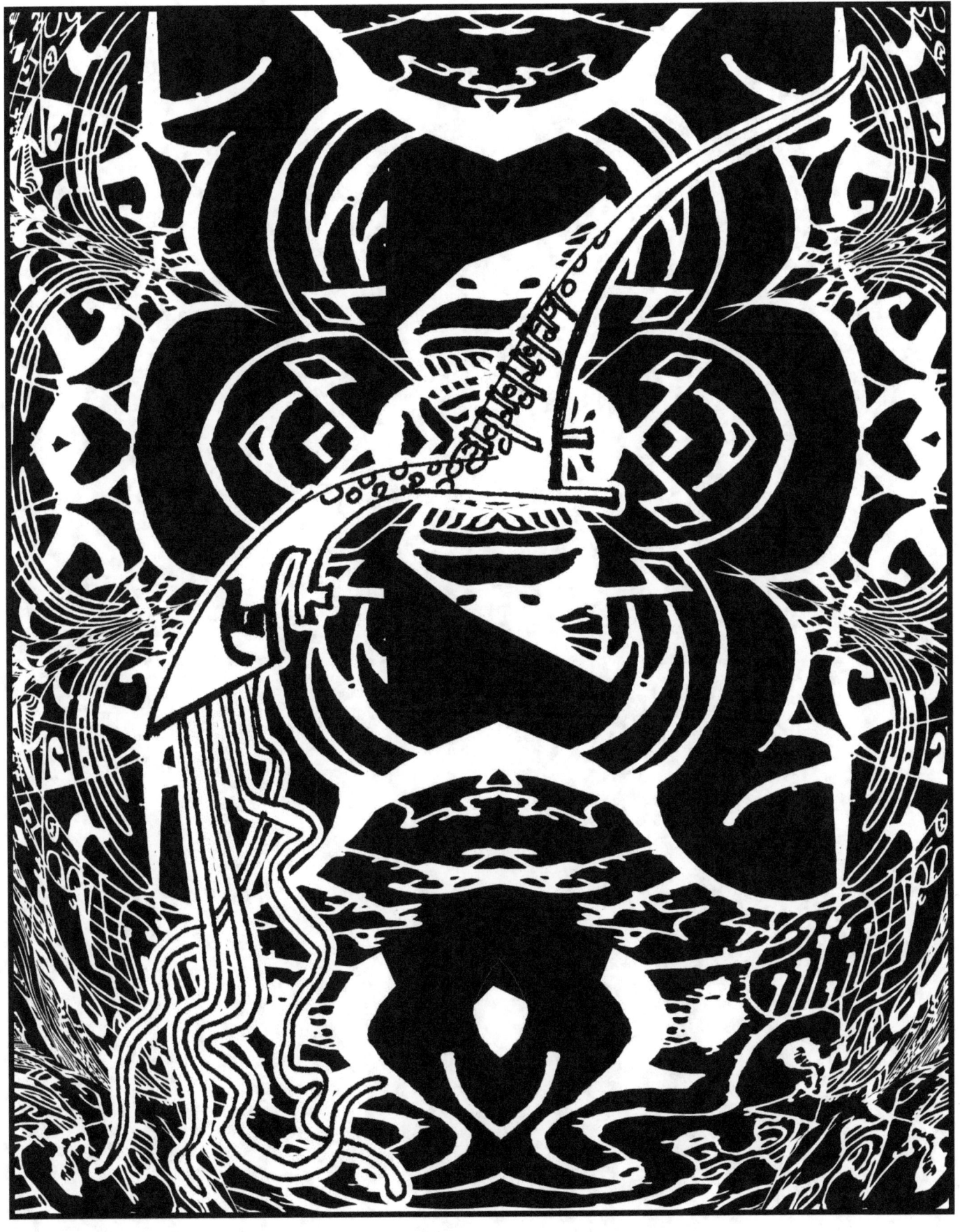

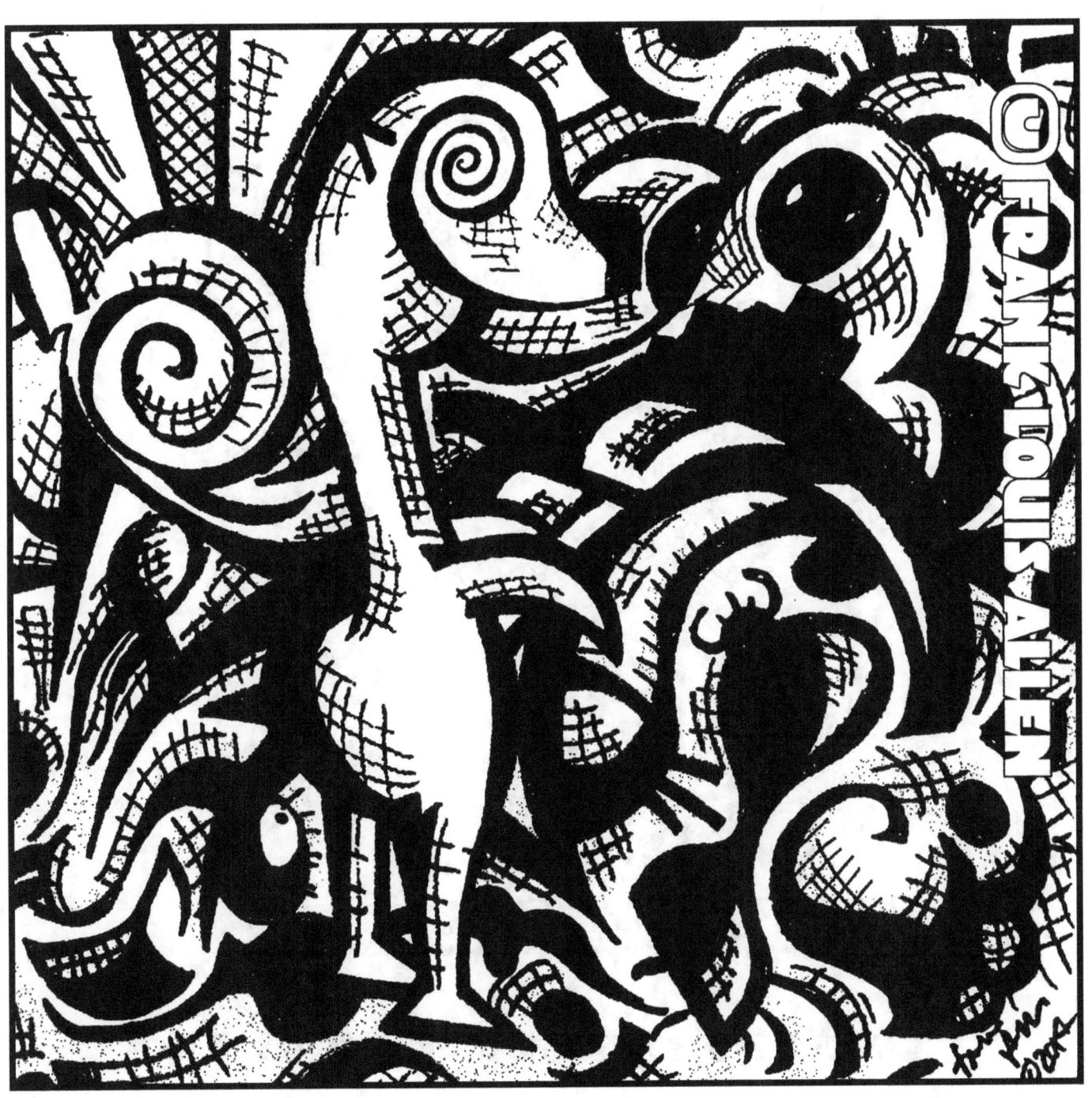

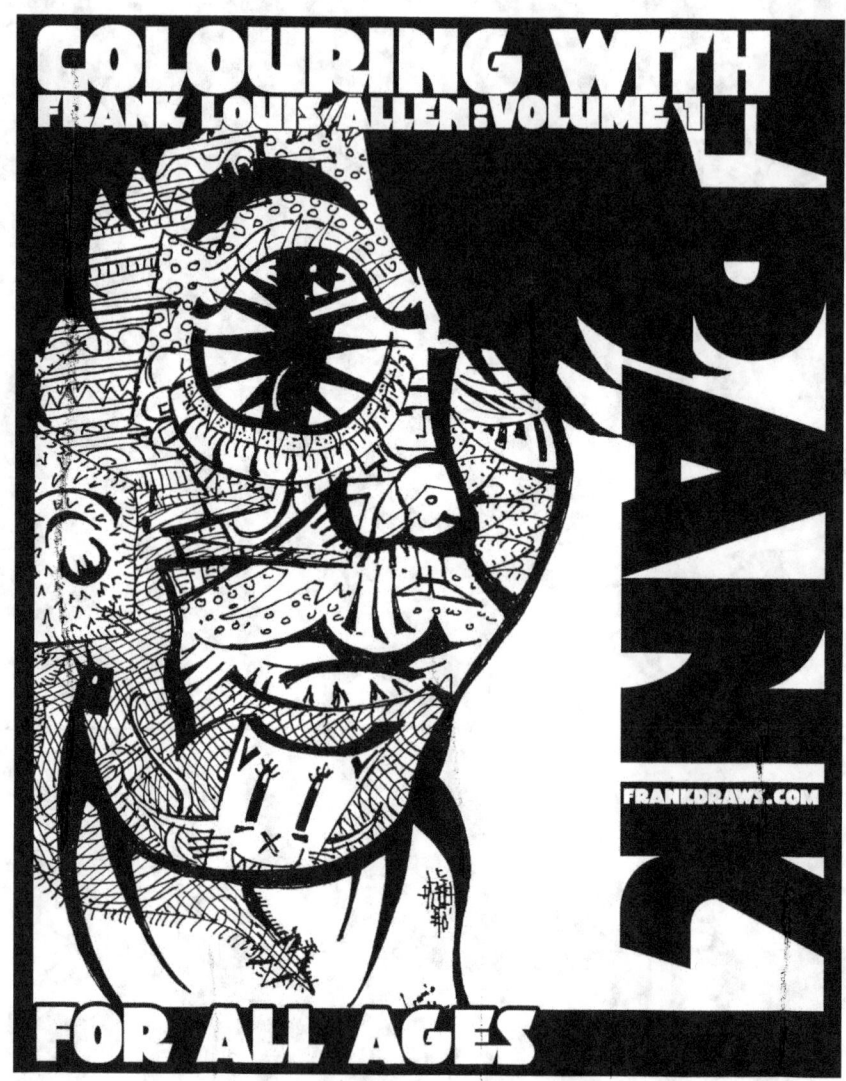

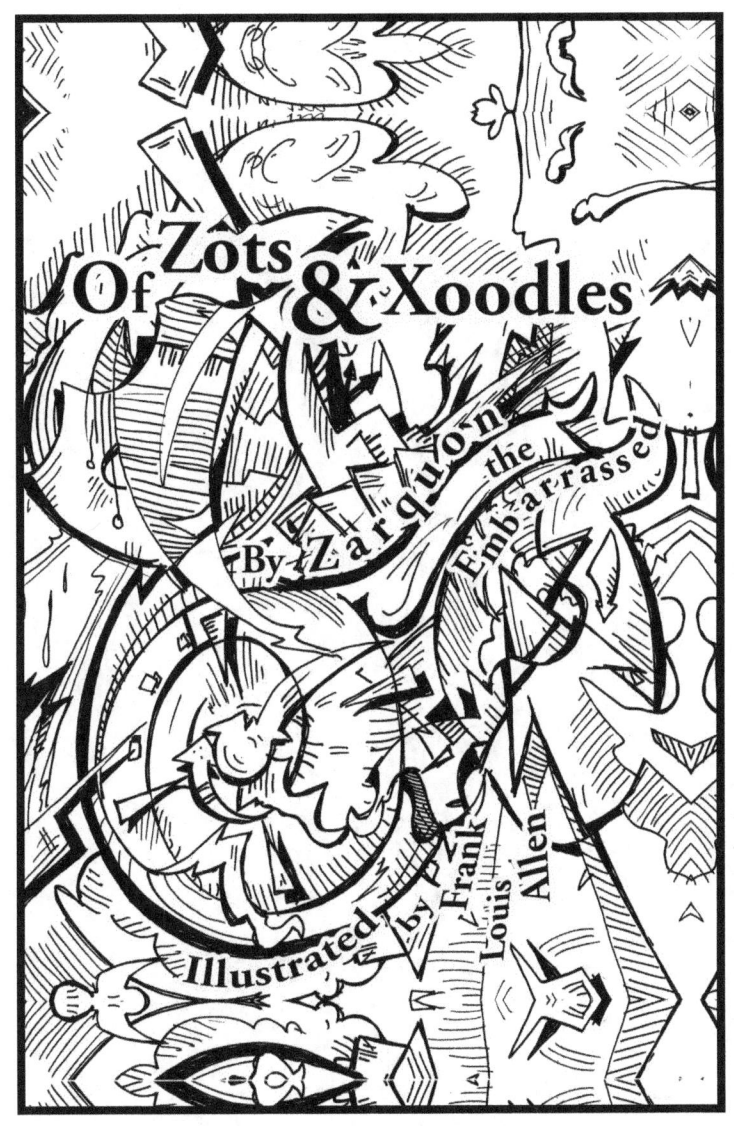

## Of Zots and Xoodles

Written by Zarquon the Embarassed

and Illustrated by Frank Louis Allen.

Dr Suess meets Dali and quantum physics

for the creation of a universe

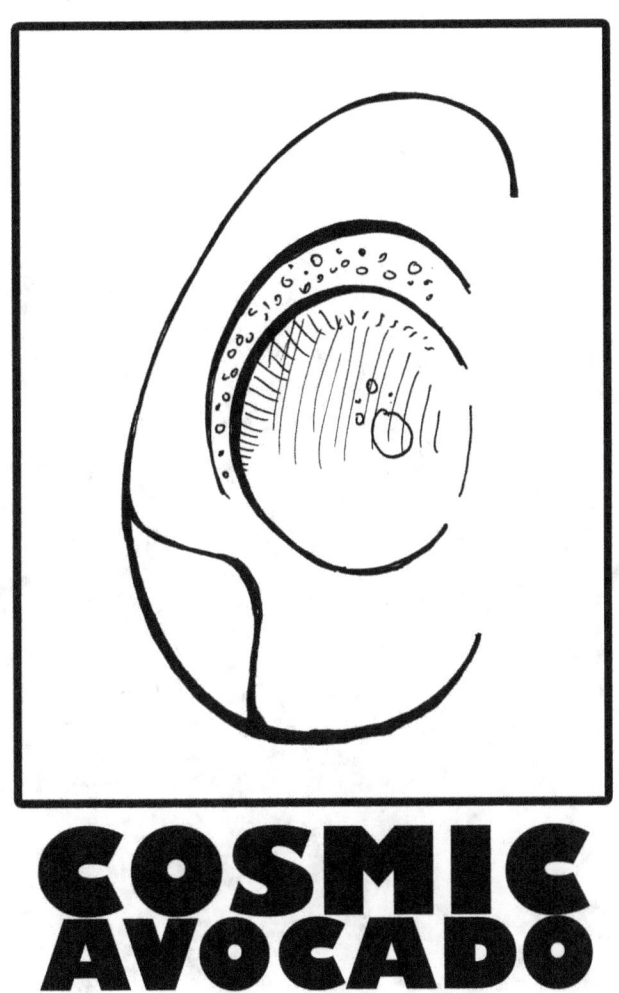

# COSMIC
# AVOCADO

**Find more books by Frank Louis Allen and his design
company Cosmic Avocado on his website as well as prints
and merchandise.**

**WWW.FRANKDRAWS.COM**

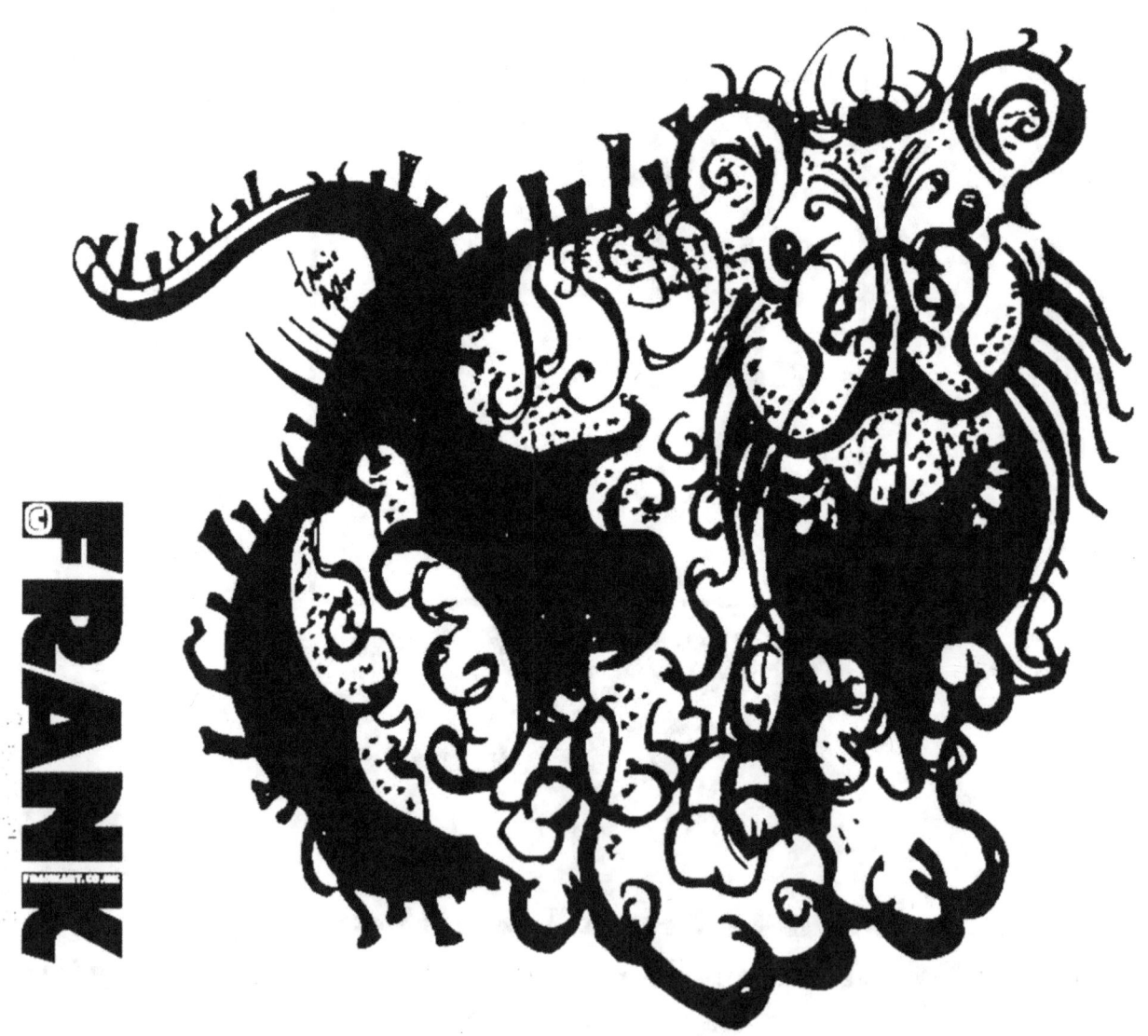

FRANK

FRANKART.CO.UK

www.ingramcontent.com/pod-product-compliance
Lightning Source LLC
Chambersburg PA
CBHW082008230526
45468CB00023B/2829